Routledge Revivals

CRIME AND PUNISHMENT
IN
GERMANY

CRIME AND PUNISHMENT IN GERMANY

THEODOR HAMPE

Routledge
Taylor & Francis Group

First published in 1929 by George Routledge & Sons, LTD.

This edition first published in 2018 by Routledge
2 Park Square, Milton Park, Abingdon, Oxon, OX14 4RN
and by Routledge
711 Third Avenue, New York, NY 10017

Routledge is an imprint of the Taylor & Francis Group, an informa business

© 1929 Taylor & Francis

Publisher's Note
The publisher has gone to great lengths to ensure the quality of this reprint but
points out that some imperfections in the original copies may be apparent.

Disclaimer
The publisher has made every effort to trace copyright holders and welcomes
correspondence from those they have been unable to contact.
A Library of Congress record exists under ISBN: 30008701

ISBN 13: 978-1-138-55408-5 (hbk)
ISBN 13: 978-0-8153-6890-8 (pbk)
ISBN 13: 978-1-351-25364-2 (ebk)

CRIME AND PUNISHMENT
IN GERMANY

VIEW OF NUREMBERG ABOUT 1520
Coloured Woodcut by Hans Wurm. Nuremberg. Germanic Museum

THEODOR HAMPE

CRIME AND PUNISHMENT
IN GERMANY

As illustrated by the
NUREMBERG MALEFACTORS' BOOKS

*Translated, with an Introduction based on Wm. Smith's
' Breeff Description of Norenberg ' (1594) by*

MALCOLM LETTS
F.S.A.

LONDON
GEORGE ROUTLEDGE & SONS, LTD.
BROADWAY HOUSE : 68-74, CARTER LANE, E.C.
1929

PRINTED IN GREAT BRITAIN BY HEADLEY BROTHERS,
18, DEVONSHIRE STREET, E.C.2 ; AND ASHFORD, KENT.

CONTENTS

CONTENTS

LIST OF ILLUSTRATIONS

LIST OF ILLUSTRATIONS

TRANSLATOR'S PREFACE

This is a translation of a work by Dr. Theodor Hampe, Director of the Germanic Museum at Nuremberg, published in 1927, entitled : *Die Nürnberger Malefizbücher als Quellen der reichstädtischen Sittengeschichte vom 14, bis zum 18. Jahrhundert (Neujahrsblätter herausgegeben von der Gesellschaft für Fränkische Gescllichte*, Heft XVII), Bamberg : C. C. Buchners Verlag.

I desire to express my thanks to Dr. Hampe for much help in dealing with difficult points, and for facilitating the reproduction of the drawings appearing in his sources ; to Dr. Altmann, keeper of the Nuremberg State Archives, for introducing me to Pfinzing's drawing of the town here reproduced ; and to the Editor of the *Times Literary Supplement* for kind permission to reprint some portions of a review of Dr. Hampe's book which appeared in his columns.

My introduction is based largely on William Smith's *Breeff Description of the Famous and Bewtifull Cittie of Norenberg*, 1594, preserved in the Lambeth Palace Library. The Rev. Claude Jenkins, Lambeth Librarian, was kind enough to facilitate the copying of the MS., and to obtain the necessary permission for the drawings to be photographed. One of these drawings is reproduced here, and I hope to return to this interesting MS. again.

A few notes have been added, mainly for the benefit of English readers who may not be familiar with Dr. Hampe's subject, or with Nuremberg. These are marked by square brackets.

MALCOLM LETTS.

TRANSLATOR'S INTRODUCTION

WE have heard a good deal lately concerning Meister Franz Schmidt, the Nuremberg executioner, who left behind him an interesting and very curious diary. Dr. Hampe, who has long been busy among the Nuremberg archives, now introduces us to other records of the gallows and the sword which add considerably to our knowledge of the administration of criminal justice in the past, and help us to understand many matters which were beyond the scope of Meister Franz's inquiries and comprehension. As the reader will see from Dr. Hampe's Introduction, Nuremberg has a wonderful collection of criminal records. There is a whole series of official registers, which may conveniently be grouped together under the head of Malefactors' Books, as well as several important collections of an unofficial nature, such as the memoranda kept by the notary Frommoder, and, above all, the Memorial of the prison chaplain Magister Johann Hagendorn, whose activities fall between the years 1605 and 1620.

It is Hagendorn's Memorial which will, I think, make the greatest appeal to the reader, for in it we see the whole business of justice in an important centre such as Nuremberg, nor from the point of view of justice, but of the church. The chaplain cared little for the crime for which the victim was to suffer, but he was deeply concerned that the wretched creature should stammer out a psalm and die with a text on his lips. A defiant attitude on the scaffold left him speechless with horror, and so earnest was he in the performance of his duties that a rogue, a Catholic, who desired time to consider the merits of the Reformed Religion and to study the Evangelists and taste their sweetness, could easily beguile him into procuring a postponement of the sentence. There are many attractive traits in Magister Hagendorn's character. He is honest, a little jealous, perhaps of his colleague Magister Lüder, and a good deal concerned for forms and ceremonies, but a thoroughly honest and upright man, whose ministrations must have comforted the last hours of many a wretched victim of justice.

But it is not my intention to anticipate Dr. Hampe in his study of social life at Nuremberg as reflected in the criminal records of the sixteenth and seventeenth centuries. The object of this introduction is to present to the reader an interesting and hitherto unknown description of Nuremberg, written by an Englishman who was living in the city at the very time when Magister Hagendorn was preparing for his ministrations among the condemned criminals. This was William Smith, later Rouge Dragon Pursuivant, a remarkable man with a doubtful temper, a sharp tongue, and the ability to draw the most delightful pictures of cities. He was a Cheshire man, born apparently somewhere about 1550. He seems to have studied at Brasenose, and after 1568 to have settled in Nuremberg where he married the daughter of a citizen called Altensteg, and kept an inn known as The Goose. Twenty years later he returned to England, and in 1597 he was created Rouge Dragon Pursuivant, which office he held until his death in 1618. He is known chiefly as the author of the 'Description of England, 1588', now in the British Museum, which was privately printed in 1879, with coloured reproduction of a whole series of charming views of the towns and cities described. Another work of his, *A Breeff Description of the Famous and Bewtifull Cittie of Norenberg*, is preserved in the Lambeth Palace Library (MS. No. 508), a beautifully-written little quarto volume with a map of the district, a view of the city, here reproduced, and coloured drawings of the coats of arms of the leading Nuremberg citizens. The work is dedicated to Lord Burghley, Lord High Treasurer of England.

In his dedication Smith is anxious to make it clear that he does not attempt a topographical description of Nuremberg, and that he cannot write so largely as he could have wished : 'for the noble and worthy Senators of this Cittie are very Jealouse, and will not suffer any Description either of their Cittie or Countrie'. He therefore confines himself to an account of their open ceremonies and customs which he thinks most worthy to be commended. As a result, we have a remarkably interesting and well informed account of the government of Nuremberg at a time when it was an important and self-governing community, with a more than paternal interest in the well-being, the expenditure, the clothes, the merrymakings, and the morals of the good people who dwelt within its walls.

Smith opens with a short account of the situation of the city :

' although it do lye in a Sandy ground, yet very delightfull, Compassed round about with Pleasant woods, and hath a very holesome ayre. And replenished with Cuning Artificers of fyne workes, which are carried into all places of the world. By which meanes the Cittie is furnished with such store of Marchants that it is a comon proverb in Germany, *The Marchants of Norenberg, the Lordes of Ulm*, and *the Citizens of Augspurg*. Also there is a Ryme which is to say in English : *The Norenborow hand, Deceaveth every land* ' (fo. 1a).

At this time Nuremberg was still to a large extent in the heyday of its prosperity, and evidence of wealth was everywhere. The burghers, as they grew rich, embellished their town with lovely houses, stonefronted, with spacious courts and lofty galleries richly decorated within and without.

' And most part not only fayre painted over ; But also their gutters and ye spoutes which carrieth the Rayne Water from ye gutters are of Copper, fashioned Lyke flying Dragons and gilded with gold. Their Buildings are very high and stately, and yet but iiii Stories (for more they may not be suffred to build), although they have comonly 3 or 4 garretts one above

6

VIEW OF NUREMBERG, 1594
By William Smith.   Lambeth Palace Library

[to face p.

another, wherein the Richer sort have their provision of Corne, And throughout all the Cittie a man shall not lightly fynd a house all of Timber, But that two of ye lowest stories are all of Stone, or the lowermost of all at the least ' (fo. 8).

Great care was exercised to see that the city was kept clean and sweet.

' It hath 528 Streets and Lanes, that are paved, 118 wells of pure water, which are builded with pillers of stone, chaynes and Bucketts, besides 14 conduits of water wherewithall almost every mans house is served. Which streets are both fayre and broad. And not only are alwaies cleane by reason of the sandy ground, but are also cleanly kept, for they have no doung hills in all their streets but in certayne odd by corners. Neither is it ye custome there to make water in the streets, or to throw out any urine before tenne of the clock at night. The punishment whereof is 20 Dollars besydes emprisonment. Yea, so precise are they in ye sweet keeping of their Cittie that although a man have a yard or backsyde in his house (as commonly they most part have), yet may he not kepe any swyne, but only one pigg, and yet that no Longer till it be half a yeare old, but have houses of purpose without ye Cittie ' (fo. 7a).

There were four great clocks and three small ones, seven bridges of stone and four of timber, thirteen hills and thirteen baths or common hot-houses. The towers were always a matter of wonder to travellers, although they could never agree as to their number. The Nuremberg Chronicle gives 365, the same number as there are days in the year, but the compiler seems to have relied on his calendar rather than on the evidence of his senses. Smith gives 183, which is probably nearer the mark. In each was a lodging for the watchman, and all through the night a man went his rounds,

7

blowing with a horn or cornet at the foot of each, to make sure that the watchman was awake. If no reply was received the culprit was sent to prison for eight days on a diet of bread and water (fo. 6a).

Of the gates and defences Smith writes as follows :

'It hath vi great gates and ii small. These gates, winter and somer, are alwaies opened an houre before sonne ryssing, and shutt alwaies an houre after Sunne going downe. The castlegate only excepted, which is opened an houre Later, and shutt an houre sooner then the other, to say when the sunne ryseth and setteth. At ech of these gates is a great Round Toure of Stone, very strong and high withal. On ye topp whereof (since of late yeares) do lye certaine cast peeces of Ordynance. And on the topp of ech of ye said Toures is a fyne Lodging for the watchman that dwelleth therein, who day and night watcheth, giving warning by sound of Trumpett when any Troupes of Horsemen or Coaches do come. And do sound also at the opening and shutting of the gates, which being once shutt are not opened for any mans pleasure ' (fo. 6a).

It was the opinion of the world at large that no town could ever approach Nuremberg in matters of government. The control of affairs generally was in the hands of a Patrician class which elected itself, and formed a species of town aristocracy from which the ordinary citizens were excluded. This led at Nuremberg, as elsewhere, to violent conflicts between the rulers and the ruled, and the Patricians had more than one narrow escape, but they contrived to retain their grip on affairs, and were never really disturbed until the beginning of the nineteenth century. Smith shared the general approbation :

8

'This Cittie is governed by a prudent and Sage Counsell, and of the Gentility aforesaid, named in Latin Patricii (for such great respect they have to their Stockes or famylies of generosity that they take no other into Counsell, be he never so Wyse, Rich, aged, Learned or come of noble Linage). Through whose politike and wise government the people are kept in quietness, dew aw and obeysance. For I think there is not a Cittie in the world where the People are more civill. As I remember I have read that about 100 yeares past one of the Cheiffest Potentates in Germany came to this Cittie, and demanding of Anthony Tucher, then one of the Cheiff Governors, how he could kepe his People so quyet, being so great a multitude, He answered, with cherishing of the good and punishing of the evell ' (fo. 10).

Then follows a long account of the system of government and election to the council, the duties and privileges of the Losunger, the alte Genannten (the 'Oldnamed'), the 'Yea Lords' ('for whatever the rest of the Lords do agree uppon, these do say yea '), the burgomasters, the magistrates, and the elders, all part of a rather complicated system which need not detain us at the moment, since the whole subject has been examined and explained by Mr. K. R. Greenfield in his excellent study of the *Nuremberg Sumptuary Laws*, published by the Johns Hopkins Press at Baltimore in 1918.

It is interesting to have a glimpse in Smith's words (Smith being himself an inn keeper) of the hospitality shown by the council to strangers :

'Every one that is an Inholder hath speciall comaundment that when any guest cometh with two horses or above, that he present his name in wryting to ye Magistrates who Immediately do send one with certain potts of wyne, who

9

sayeth these wordes in effect, *Honorable or Worshipfull &c. My lordes, the Magistrates of this Cittie, have with great Joy understood of your Honors coming to Towne, And in token of their good will, they present you with these fewe pottes of Wyne, which they pray you to take in good part (or if he be a great parsonage, he sayeth) Praying you to continew their gratious and favourable good Lord. . . .* If he be a prince or such Lyke, then they send hym a whole wagon Laden with wyne, another with otes and provender, and ye third with fish and other victualls ' (fo. 14).

Before turning to the other activities of the council it may be interesting to have Smith's report on the integrity of the Nuremberg citizens as a whole.

' So trew and Just are they in their dealings that their word is as much as an obligation. In so much that at a fayre tyme some one man shall deale fore 20, 30 or 40 thousand pounds English mony uppon Creditt, without making any bill or obligation. Yea, some of them and most part will bring home their mony the same day it is dew or beffore, because he will not have it reported that he paid after his day. So trew and Just are they that if you lose a purse with money in the street, Ring bracelet or such Lyke, you shalbe sure to have it again. I would it were so in London ' (fo. 14a-15).

Excellent as the government of Nuremberg seems to have been, it must he admitted that the council interfered fairly extensively with the private affairs of the citizens. The authorities required them not only to carry on their trades in accordance with official standards of right and wrong, but to adjust their personal expenditure, to dress, eat, marry and even to die according to rule. The authorities enquired into the expenditure upon weddings, christenings, burials, bathing parties, feasts, gifts and displays of

every kind. No one could become secretly betrothed.
The ceremony had to be performed openly at the
Rathaus in the presence of witnesses. Sixteen witnesses
were allowed for each party and no more, but after the
official business, the groom might send a company of
friends, fixed by law at seventeen, to wish the bride
happiness, and these she might entertain with Rhine
wine or wine of a similar grade or quality. A further
visit of congratulation by twenty-four women followed,
and on the evening of the betrothal the bride and groom
might entertain four friends to dinner, but the ladies
of the party were on no account to stay all night. If
the lover desired to serenade his lady, the refreshment
to be offered to the musicians was restricted to fruit,
cheese and bread, to be passed round once only, with a
discreet measure of inexpensive wine. The groom
might give his lady a silver brooch with a chain, the
value of which was strictly limited, and a ring which,
with the stones, was not to cost more than from ten
to fifteen gulden. In return he could receive a shirt,
a bath-suit, and bonnet of prescribed value. So with
weddings. The number of guests, the food and drink,
the merry-making and the fooling were all prescribed,
with penalties for breach of the regulations. At
dinner, partridge, hazel-hen, pheasant, grouse, peacock,
capon (whether toast or boiled), venison, heron, fish,
and wedding herbs were all excluded, and neither
spiced wine nor serenade money was to be bestowed.
Feasts and merrymakings by the newly-married couple

were restricted to one wedding party in the new home with seven guests, and when the time came for a christening a whole set of fresh regulations had to be mastered, while the burial ordinances would need a chapter to themselves.[1] Small wonder if Smith is constrained to remark that the people of Nuremberg went decently and orderly to their festivities and to church 'not in heaps lyke a flock of sheepe as in London' (fo. 18a). After they had read and mastered the Hochzeitsbüchlein, or Wedding Manual, issued by the authorities, together with the countless other regulations, and had further submitted their wardrobes and personal accounts for inspection, they can have had little spirit left for ordinary enjoyment and merry-making.

This is Smith's account of their marriages and christenings :

'If any do Contract Matrimony without Consent of their Parentes or frendes, then ar the Parentes not bound to geve any thing with them. Such marriages ar called Corne Marriages. But the comon and right maner of Proceeding therein is thus. First he that is to be married sendeth 3 or 4 of his Chieffest frendes to ye fathers house of the Damsell, to Demand her in marriage. Who beinge brought into a Parlar, There doth as many of her frends stand on ye other syde of the parlor. And then one of his frendes sayeth in effect as followeth. *Worshippfull Sirs, our Kinsman & frend N. desyreth your daughter, or neece &c. to be geven hym in laufull matrimony. Wherefore we pray you of your favourable & determinate answers.* Then doth her frends Comonly desyre

[1] See *Sumptuary Law at Nuremberg*, by Dr. K. R. Greenfield (Johns Hopkins University Studies, 1918).

12

3 Weekes or a months respyte, to conferre with the rest of
their frends, who peradventure are out of Towne, or with
the maid her selff, who oftetimes knoweth nothing of ye
matter till they have concluded, which in my opinion is not
to be Comended. But being once agreed, They send for ye
Bryde, whom the Brydgrome taketh by ye hand, And
Immediatly all the kindred (so many as is there present) do
also geve them their handes, wishing them Joye.

Then are ye Covenants drawne out in wryting, sealed
with two of ye Comon Counsell, And ye day of Marriage
agreed uppon, which marriage dayes, are alwase on Mondais,
Tewsdais, or Wensdaies.

Six dayes beffore ye marriage, They wryte upp the names
of all those which they will have bidden to ye wedding, And
Deliver ye same to one whose office is to bidd to weddings
and Burialls (whereof there is about 12 in all). This man
goeth in stately maner, with a man waiting on him, from one
to another, noting all them that promise to come, till he
have his Just nomber. For above 60 there may not come
to supper, which is V tables & 12 at every table. But to
go to church with them they may have as many as they will,
or can gett to come. And therfore when there is a man &
his wyffe bidden to ye marriage (for they odd none but
maried folkes), Comonly they go both of them to ye Church,
& but one of them to ye feast, which is alwaies a Supper.
The wordes which the wedding bidder speaketh, are these
in effect. *Worshippfull Sir I am sent vnto you, by ye ii
fathers, N.W. & R.C. with ye Brydegrome F.D. And the
Verteous Maid M.K. his bethroathed Bryde, who most earnestly
pray & desire you and your Bedfellow, on tewsday next to go
with them to ye Christian Church, to ye Solemniation of their
marriage, which shalbe at ye Church of St. G. at service tyme.
And moreover they pray you both that you will honor them with
your presente at supper the same day at night, which supper
shalbe kept in ye house of D.L. at vi of ye Clock. In Recompence whereof ye said parents Brydegrome & Bryde wilbe redy
at all tymes to do the Lyke for you or yours.* When the day of
marriage is come, certaine of the neerest frendes are bidd
home in ye morning to Breakfast, which done they go into

ye Church (I meane the men only), And in ye Middest of ye Church the Brydegrome standeth betwene ye two fathers, till all they that be bidden be come. Who coming first to ye Brydegrome, do take him by the hand, saying, *I wish you good fortune to ye holy estate of matrimony.* And then Immediatly taking ye fathers also by the hand, do say, *I wish you good fortune, to your new kindred.* When they be all come together, then do they go in comely & decent order, iii & iii in a Ranck, & fetch the Bryde, who cometh forth with all ye women after her, iii & iii in a ranck. And on ech side of her a maid, all three in very costly Apparell, & garlands of pearle on their bare heads. But if she be one of the gentility, then hath she a Coronall of gold on her head, & is ledd betwene two of the Magistrates. Being come near vnto ye Church, they that kepe watch in the Steple do sound their trompetts. And so Likewise when they go back againe. So soone as they be come into ye Church they are presently maried. And after some musike & playing on ye organes they retorne againe in ye same order, till they come to ye house dore, where they stay, and lett ye Bryde & the women go in. Then do ye 2 fathers thanck the rest of the men in this maner followinge. *Worshippfull Sirs. We two fathers, Brydegrome, Bryde, and ye whole kindred, do thanck your Worships for your paines taking in going with vs to the Holy Church. Being alwaies redy to recompence the same wherein we may or shalbe able.*

The same night, after supper is finished, they have Dancing till 10 of ye Clock (for longer they may not be suffred). And so ye first day of the Wedding is accomplished. The second day at night They bidd certaine Batchelors & Maids, and the Cheiffest of their frendes or kindred to supper, And have dancing againe till ten of the clock, And then it is wholy finished' (fo. 17a-19).

' *Of their Christnings*

At their Christnings they use not many Ceremonies, for commonly there goeth none but Women and Children to ye Church with the Chyld. The Children go beffore, and next beffore the Midwyffe (who carrieth ye Chylde) goeth

14

a little boy, if it be a man chyld, or a girl, if it be a Wench, bearing a stick made and paynted Lyke a Taper of Wax. After the Christning (which is alwaies at two of the clock in ye afternoon) Then They have a Banket, and so that matter is finished also. But here in this Country, if it be a boy, then they have but one godfather, and to a girle but one godmother. The women do lye 6 weekes in chyldbedd, and then go alone to ye Church without any other Company or any other adoe ' (fo. 19a).

Smith is equally detailed in his description of burials. Here again the council stepped in and controlled any temptation to extravagance. The amount of wax to be spent on candles, the number of mourners, the cost of the pall, and of the memorials, were all strictly limited, and no one might hang up in a church or convent a shield for the dead of greater size or weight than was prescribed and fixed in the measurements given to the churchmasters of St. Lawrence's and St. Sebald's. Smith gives us the form of the expression of condolence (' I am sorry for your heaviness '), the order of the procession, and ends with the remarks that ' so all is finished without any banketing or feasting ' (fo. 20a-21).

If in their attitude to private affairs the city fathers were inclined to be inquisitive and dictatorial, it must be admitted that in matters affecting the community at large they were both far-sighted and broad-minded. They looked after the sick and poor, prescribed the times when charity children might beg and sing psalms in public, policed the streets, issued building regulations, contrived some system of land registration, and administered the finances of the town with wisdom and discretion. There is no space to give Smith's description of much else concerning the government of the city, but his accounts of the provision for the poor and sick, and of the elaborate precautions which were taken for dealing with outbreaks of fire, a constant source of danger to crowded communities, contain some interesting facts, not, as far as I know, to be found elsewhere.

' Of their Provisyon for the Poore

' Besydes dyvers Almes houses and their goodly faire & large new Hospital, they do give a weekly Almes to ye poore, for none may be suffred to begg within ye Cittie, neither yong nor old. And whereas there are many poore Children which go to scoole, and were alwaies wont, at noone tyme & at night, to begg in the streetes at every mans dore with singing of psalmes, now there is such order taken that they do only every Monday, Wensday & Fryday go along through ye streets singing, two of them carring of baskets wherein they put ye bread which is geven them, and other two have boxes wherein they put their mony ' (fo. 21a).

' Provision for the Sick.

Less then a quarter of an English Myle from ye Cittie (which is of like distance that their Buriall places are) is the goodly new buildings called *The Lazaret*, furnished throughout with severall fayre roumes, Bedds, Cleane Linnen, Doctors, Surgions, women to attend the Sick, fresh fountains of water, besydes the ronning River hard by, and all other things thereunto belonging; That it is seldome seene that any dyeth that is brought thither, but so soone as he is well recovered, then he goeth home agayne to his owne house.[1]

Such Lyke Lazaret have I often wished, as is now in building in the feildes betwene London & Islington. I pray God it may come to some good Effect '.

[1] The account of the hospital scarcely accords with the story related by Dr. Hampe at p. 69.

' Provision for Defence of Fyre

This is worthy the noting, that when any house chanceth to be on fyre (yea, although it be but a chimney) and that ye flame is seene to ryse iii foot high, Then do they which kepe watch smyte the Laram belles. The Towne gates are shutt, And all the Cittie vpp in Armour, with their Captains and all other furniture thereunto belonging, placed in Battail array as if the Enemie were already entred. He that is first on horseback in any of the 4 market places hath 100 florins, the second 50, the third 25, & all the rest 6 florins a peece. Every man knoweth what he hath to do. Those which carry water, Ladders & Bucketts are ye Carmen & Porters of ye Cittie, who are sworne thereunto when they are first admitted to be Porters. He that bringeth the first Ladder or fyre hook hath a florin, the second half a florin, the third a quarter, and all ye rest the sixt part of a florin a peece. And so lykewise he that bringeth ye first tubb with water, or Buckett. No man nedeth to trouble him selff further then his charge is. They ronne not on heapes as they do in London, without either rule or order ' (fo. 22).

Smith now turns to the administration of justice, and his notes provide an interesting supplement to much that Dr. Hampe has to tell us. It is difficult to avoid the conclusion that at Nuremberg, as elsewhere in the sixteenth and seventeenth centuries, malefactors had very short shrift. The procedure becomes fairly clear from Dr. Hampe's pages. As I understand the matter, the accused was first allowed to tell his own story. Then he was pressed by the prison magistrate with a series of searching questions, after which, if still obdurate, he was tortured until he named his accomplices and confessed, and on that confession he was executed. A trial, as we understand it, did not

17

exist. The law required that the evidence of guilt should be clearer than the light, and nothing could be clearer than confession, by whatever means it was obtained. The system exhibits all the worst features of the inquisitorial, as opposed to the accusatory, procedure. It was secret, the accused had practically no opportunity for defence, and judgment was already decided upon before the hearing, which was little better than an empty form. Once a suspect passed into the hands of the law his situation was indeed a desperate one.

Another thing which strikes us as we read these and other criminal records is the horror which seized the most abandoned criminals at the prospect of being hanged. They were ready, may be, to die, but would move heaven and earth to obtain the privilege of losing their heads. Magister Hagendorn records again and again with what rapture the victims received the news that, after all, they were not to swing, but might die honourably by the sword. They cried with joy, and kissed his hands, and fell upon their knees and praised God. There is no doubt that the malefactor's horror was rooted in the fact that, after hanging, the bodies were left swinging from the gallows, while the corpses, after decapitation, were decently disposed of ; but the whole attitude displays a sensitiveness not easily to be reconciled with other records of the period.

Smith is on the whole correct in his remarks and deductions, but the poisoned rod has not come under

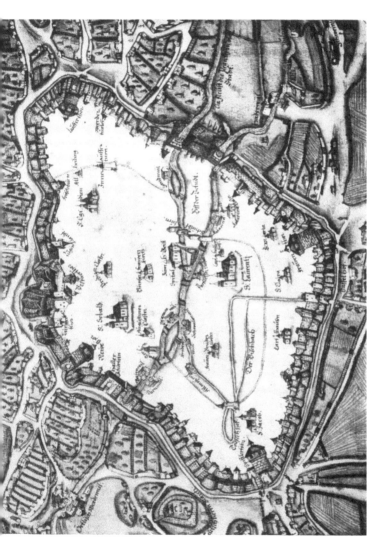

VIEW OF NUREMBERG ABOUT 1594
By Paulus Pfinzing. State Archives, Nuremberg

[to face p. 18

my notice previously, and I am inclined to regard it as a myth.

' *Punishment of Malefactors*

Every one that is brought into prison for any matter worthy of death is beffore two of ye Magistrates racked, & his Confession taken in wryting. During ye time he lyeth in prison they wryte to other Citties, Letting them vnderstand that they have such a one in hold, & what he hath confessed. Sometimes there cometh more matter from other places. Three daies beffore ye execution he hath warning geven him to prepare him selff to dye. During which iii daies there is alwaies a preacher with him, is watched day & night, and hath geven hym whatsoever he desyreth, either of meat or drink. When the day of execution cometh (which is alwais on a Tewsday or Thursday) He is brought beffore the Judge, who sitteth with a whyte rodd in his right hand, and with his left hand holdeth a short two hand sword, with a paire of gantletts hanging at the Crosse, and about 12 of ye magestrates, to say, on each hand vi. Then is his Confession redd by the Clarke, at the later end whereof, is written thus : *Which being against ye lawes of the Holy Romish Empire, my Lordes have decreed and geve sentence that he shalbe, &c.* Then doth ye Judge ask every one of ye Lordes particularly, begining with the yongest first, saying : *Sir N. how doth the Sentence please you ?* Who answereth *What Law & Justice is, pleaseth me.* Then doth the Judge say thus to ye Hangman. *Executioner, I comaund thee in ye name of ye holy Romish Empire, that thou carry him to ye place of execution &c.* And so he is presently caried to ye gallows, which is about a flight shoot from ye Cittie.

If it be for theft, then he is hanged. Yet a Citezen hath such favour shewed him that he is beheaded with the Sword. For murther, pinched with hott glowing tonges, & broken with the wheele. He that setteth any mans house, barne or stable on fyre, is burned. The women are for all offences whatsoever drowned, except Witches. He that sweareth a false oath hath the two ioynts of his formost fingers cutt of & cast into ye River. He that blasphemeth God hath the

19

end of his tongue cut out & cast into the River. Other offences, which be not so haynous, The offenders are only whipped out of ye Towne with a Rodd by the Hangman & banished. But sometymes the offence is such that the Rodd is poysined, and he whipped in such sort that he liveth not long after.'

There is a great deal more in Smith's description which is of interest to the student of Nuremberg's past, such as lists of the councillors from 1477 to 1591, the oaths taken on election, and the special duties performed by the city officials. Unfortunately Smith does not give us the names of the inns (Dr. Hampe supplies the deficiency in Appendix IV), but he provides a list of the common baths : the Rose Bath, Zacharias Bath, Sunn Bath, Sand Bath, Shambles Bath, Spring Bath, Strawsack Bath, Sadler's Bath, to name a few only, and he ends with eleven pages of coats of arms preceded by the following note : ' Such as be Desyrous to know the Armes of the Gentility of the Cittie, as well those which remayne yet alive, as such also which be dead (whereof some are quyte extinct), shall fynd the same hereafter in their Right Coulers, after the Order of the Alphabeth &c.' I wish I could reproduce them and print much else, but I have already kept the reader too long from Dr. Hampe's learned and interesting, if rather grim, study.

AUTHOR'S PREFACE

FOR more than a year I have been presenting both
verbally and in print the results of my studies of the
Nuremberg Malefactors' Books, or rather of crime,
punishment and execution as reflected in the official
and private records of Nuremberg during the centuries
when it was a free Imperial city. An address in
September, 1925, on the occasion of the diet at Rabisbon
of the Gesamtverein der deutschen Geschichts-und
Altertumsvereine, and another at Lindau, at the
meeting of the association of the Bayr. Geschichts-und
Urgeschichtsvereine, which dealt specifically with
matters of folklore, are to be found in extended form
in the periodical *Bayerischer Heimatschutz* published
by the Bayr. Landesverein für Heimatschutz, Verein
für Volkskunst und Volkskunde in München (21
Jahrgang, 1925, pp. 52ff). A further contribution,
based on the same abundant material, was published
in the Mitteilungen des Vereins für Geschichte der
Stadt Nürnberg, Vol. XXVI, 1926, pp. 321ff, under
the title : *Des Nürnberger Scharfrichters Franz Schmidt
letzte Amtsverrichtung, 13 Nov.* 1617 [the last official
execution by Franz Schmidt, the Nuremberg execu-
tioner], and this essay was reprinted later in a private

and limited edition, with additions and corrections based upon subsequent and extended researches.

I should like, at the same time, to say that the indication of the value of this type of manuscript material for the study of social history, and particularly of folklore, has led to renewed study elsewhere of sources which are in no sense confined to legal history, as at Bremen and at Soest, for instance, where the so-called " Nequambücher" and their contribution to matters such as these are in question. An earlier worker with similar aims and convictions, among others, was Georg Schoppe, whose essay *Volkskunde in schlesischen Archivalien* [Folklore in Silesian archives] in the Mitteilungen der Schlesischen Gesellschaft für Volkskunde, edited by Theodor Siebs, vol. XXV (1924), pp. 79ff, dealt with the Malefactors' Books in the town archives of Breslau. It is scarcely necessary to mention that our archives have also been searched in earlier times for particular instances of this kind—I have in mind Kriegk's *Deutsches Bürgertum im Mittelalter,* which dealt specially with conditions at Frankfurt—or that much has been extracted from the literature of crime and justice for use in the study of social history. As far as Nuremberg is concerned, apart from earlier studies, for the most part limited in extent,[1] we have

---

[1] E.g., *Historischdiplomatisches Magazin für das Vaterland und angrenzende Gegenden,* vol. II. Stück 2 (Nuremberg, 1782), pp. 218ff ; Christoph Gottlieb von Murr's *Journal zur Kunstgeschichte und zur allgemeinen Literatur,* Pt. XV (1787) pp. 63ff. (Extracts from the Wandelbüchlein 1285-1335) ; Georg Ernst Waldau's *Vermischte Beyträge zur Geschichte der Stadt Nürnberg,* vol. II (1787), pp. 169ff, vol. IV (1789), pp. 345ff (dealing with the case of Nikolaus von Gülchen) ; *Neue Beiträge*

in modern times above all the work of Hermann Knapp whose study of the Lochgefängnis [the prison called the Loch] is almost exclusively a study of social history. To this should be added the manuscript Memorials of Master Franz Schmidt, for many years executioner to the Imperial city of Nuremberg,[2] together with Karl von Hegel's study of Niklas Muffel's life and death,[3] Wilhelm Fürst's essay on the crimes and execution of Nikolaus von Gülchen,[4] and my own contributions to the history of the lampoonist, Johann Philipp Andreae,[5] and the swindler Hans Vatter of Mellingen,[6] with many others. That the records which have come down to us have been imperfectly used in the past will, I think, appear, at least as far as Nuremberg is concerned, from the contents of the following pages, especially when compared with the available literature on the subject,

---

I, pp. 432ff (the prison called the Loch) ; Johann Christian Siebenkees, *Materialien zur Nürnbergischen Geschichte*, I (1792), pp. 373f. " Strenger Gerechtigkeitseifer der Nürnbergischen Bürger im vorigen Jahrhundert " (a case of lynch-justice on the traitorous messenger Simon Schiller, or Schilling in 1612 ; compare the account by Frommoder in ch. VIII below) ; II (1792) pp. 689 ff., III (1794), pp. 278ff, IV (1795), pp. 551, and many others.

[1] *Das alte Nürnberger Kriminalverfahren bis zur Einführung der Carolina*, Berlin, 1891 ; *Das alte Nürnberger Kriminalrecht*, Berlin, 1896 ; *Das Lochgefängnis, Tortur und Hinrichtung in Alt-Nürnberg*, Nuremberg, 1907.

[2] *Meister Frantzen Nachrichter albier in Nürnberg, all sein Richten am Leben*, herausgegeben von J. M. F. von Endter, Nürnberg, 1801 ; *Maister Franntzn Schmidts, Nachrichters inn Nürnberg, all sein Richten*, herausgegeben von Albrecht Keller, Leipzig, 1913 ; [English translation of part with title *A Hangman's Diary*, by C. Calvert and A. W. Gruner, London, 1928.]

[3] *Mitteilungen des Vereins für Geschichte der Stadt Nürnberg*, Heft XIV (1901), pp. 227ff.

[4] *Ibid.*, Heft XX (1913), pp. 132ff.

[5] *Ibid.*, Heft XXII (1918), pp. 244ff.

[6] *Unterhaltungsblatt des Fränkischen Kurier*, 1st, 9th, 16th and 23rd January, 1910.

a sketch of which I have already given. In view of the nature of the present publication,[1] it has been possible only to give the substance of the original authorities, an abbreviated survey, as it were, illustrated nevertheless by numerous examples from what was most valuable, not only for the science of folklore, but also for social history in general. At the same time, owing to lack of space, I have not printed voluminous extracts from official documents and other authorities in notes or appendices, but have given the substance of them in the treatise itself. I was able to venture the more readily on this course, since the language of the second half of the sixteenth and of the seventeenth centuries, which are the main periods dealt with, offer few difficulties to the general reader of to-day, and to print a modern version together with the original text would have overburdened the work unduly.

I close these prefatory notes with heartfelt thanks to the governing body (Director Dr. Altmann) and the officials of the department of the State Archives at Nuremberg, who have laboured in every way to lighten my researches among widely-placed manuscript material.

THEODOR HAMPE.

Nuremberg, in March, 1927.

---

[1] [The work appeared in *Neujahrsblätter*, herausgegeben von der Gesellschaft für fränkische Geschichte, Heft 17, 1927.]

AUTHOR'S INTRODUCTION

The Manuscripts

BEFORE proceeding to consider the facts disclosed by our sources, it is essential to glance for a moment at the manuscripts to which we owe our information, and which in the future deserve to be used much more extensively than hitherto, and to examine them in relation to each other.

When an offence came to light and the officers had succeeded in apprehending the culprit and had placed him in custody, a lengthy enquiry was instituted in the prison, or Loch, a labyrinth of cells, passages and spacious rooms beneath the Rathaus. This inquiry continued for many weeks, and during its course two of the councillors, who had been appointed to the office of prison magistrates (Lochschöffen), had to report regularly to the council as to its progress and the results obtained. The protocol containing the report of the proceedings and the evidence of the witnesses was drawn up by the prison clerk. The original reports, which were tied together in bundles at the close of the proceedings, have unfortunately only survived in a few exceptional instances. They are frequently referred to, however, in the records known as the Achtbücher, which contained summaries or extracts carefully written out in a clerkly hand for the use of the council. A "Red Book" and a "Green Book" are also referred to as the original or actual sources in the "Extracts concerning certain misdeeds" dating from the first half of the fifteenth century. The official records which have come down to us, to which belongs the oldest malefactors' book, the "Wandelbüchlein", 1285-1335, of Murr's journal (see p. 22, note 1) are not in early times of any great importance for the study of social history, and nothing like a complete series of the Achtbücher has been preserved. I am able to connect these gaps with a resolution of the council of 21 August, 1579, a copy of which, on a loose sheet of paper, has been inserted between sheets 104 and 105 in the Achtbuch of 1578-1581 (Amts-und Standbücher der Reichstadt Nürnberg [Registers of offices and rank] in the Nuremberg State Archives, MS. 209, fo.). It reads as follows :

' At a meeting of your honourable council, on the motion of Paulus Ulrichs, Haderschreiber,[1] it was announced that although it had until then been the custom, which had come down from former times, for the Urgichten upon persons awaiting judgment as set forth in the Achtbücher[2] to be written on parchment, and seeing that such books were seldom used, and that a single book costs at present no less then 30 or 40 florins, and that even so in these wretched

---

[1] [The Haderschreiber was the clerk who kept the registers of minor disputes and quarrels, and recorded the punishments inflicted.]

[2] [On the Urgicht-und Achtbücher see note at p. 38. Urgicht comes from "Ur" = from, and "jehen" = statement, and signifies statement or confession.]

times it did not last more than 8 or 10 years, whereas in the old times such a book could scarcely be filled in 30 years ; therefore in the future, with the view of saving unnecessary expense, the Achtbücher for persons awaiting judgment are to be of medium paper. Nevertheless the Urphed[1] and punishment registers, being in daily use, shall continue to be written on parchment as heretofore. Done 21 August [15]79.

Bartlme Pömer, Pieter Rieter '

The earlier volumes which were written entirely on parchment were probably discarded later, and in times of great hardship and material distress, as, for instance, when Nuremberg gave up its Imperial status and was united to the Kingdom of Bavaria, they were doubtless sold to the goldsmiths, who were always in need of parchment. In any case the Achtbücher which have come down to us begin with a stout paper volume covering the period 1578-1581 (MS. 209 Amts-und Standbücher). The codification of the actual proceedings continues down to the year 1637 (MS. 220 : 1625-1637), and this material forms naturally one of our main sources, although, as already mentioned, the Achtbücher do not contain the genuine earliest records, and in copying from other sources the writer has at times introduced misreadings, errors in transcription and mistakes of that kind.

To the Achtbücher belongs also a second series of official records dating from early times, at least for cases in which a penal judgment, e.g. a sentence of death had to be executed. These contain, for the most

---

[1] [Urphed was the oath which put an end to a dispute : oath of reconciliation.]

27

part, only the substance of the judgment which had been pronounced, and shorter or longer notices concerning the execution itself. The existence of these independent records, to which Knapp gave the name Halsgerichtsbücher [records of death sentences], may in the end have rendered superfluous the much more detailed versions contained in the Achtbücher, and may well have led to the discontinuance of the latter in the year 1637. They have been preserved from 1487 to 1743 (MS. 221-225), after which the original records seem to have been continued alone.

Many volumes, both of the Acht and Halsgerichtsbücher, are adorned with singular pen-drawings, which show the Rabenstein [the gibbet], or a poor victim, and very frequently the heads which had been severed by the sword. Some of these drawings, which are of considerable artistic merit, and which at a later date I propose to describe in greater detail with selected reproductions, may possibly have come from the pen of the well-known writing and arithmetic master Paulus Frank, who himself, it seems, only just escaped the hangman's axe at Memmingen in 1595 as a man-slayer. Frank subsequently obtained a post in the Nuremberg Council in the Chancery.[1] A whole series of codices in the Nuremberg libraries and archives at

[1] See my essay : " Initialen in Holzschnitt von dem Rechenmeister Paulus Frank um 1600,", in Mitteilungen aus dem Germanischen Nationalmuseum, 1896, pp. 49ff. [Certain of the drawings referred to by Dr. Hampe are reproduced in the following pages. I desire to express my thanks to Dr. Hampe for selecting them, and to the authorities for permission to reproduce them. They must, I think, be unique.

the turn of the century show his wonderfully clear, artistic and accomplished penmanship, which can be recognised also in the greater part of manuscript 223 (1584-1618) of the Amts-und Standbücher [registers of office and rank].   In the same way many of the pages of the last Halsgerichtsbuch which has survived (MS., 225 : 1686-1743) have been richly embellished by another artist in caligraphy with curves and spirals.

The natural complement to these official malefactors' books, is to be found in various other official reports, above all in the council registers and records, in the town accounts, and in the Haderbücher, or registers of quarrels, all of which were freely used by Knapp in his various publications.   Further information can also be obtained from numerous manuscripts of a more or less private or literary character.   Next, apart from the very informative Müllner annals[1] and other chronicles, come a number of codices which present a kind of summary of the official records throughout the centuries.   These widely-scattered extracts throw a vivid light on legal matters as affecting every class of the community, particularly the Nuremberg patriciate, and date for the most part from a time when the records of the council were much more perfect than at present.   They contain, therefore, for our purposes a mass of valuable information which is absent from the imperfect official records.   These manuscripts which may be met with, half a dozen at a time, in several

[1] [Müllner, *Annalen der Stadt Nurnberg*, Nuremberg, Town Archives.]

libraries, such as the Town Library at Nuremberg (Schwarz-Amberger Norica Collection), or in the family library of Paul Wolfgang Merkel in the Germanic Museum, as well as in many other collections (Germanic Museum, State-library at Munich, Bamberg, etc.), contain for the most part only extracts or copies made from copies, and detailed enquiry or investigation as to the sources from which the group as a whole is derived would be scarcely worth while.

Of far greater importance for the history of jurisprudence, as well as for social life, is a further group of private records which in part can be regarded as original sources. Some of these have an official character, such as the Geuder Malefactors' Book, cited frequently by Hermann Knapp (in the Geuder family archives at Heroldsberg, near Nuremberg), except that this document does not deal with judgments and punishments in Nuremberg as a whole, but only with the particular jurisdiction exercised by the Geuder family.[1]

We have next to consider the works relating to Nuremberg which take the form of memoirs. First come the records of the Nuremberg executioner Franz Schmidt, already mentioned, which have several times been printed. Schmidt filled his office for forty-four years, from 1573 to 1617. Again, Magister George Müller the Elder (1557-1619), deacon of St. Sebald's in

[1] [The Geuder Junkers were lords of Heroldsberg, near Nuremberg, and exercised jurisdiction in matters of life and death within their territory.]

INSTRUMENTS OF TORTURE AND PUNISHMENT
From Bambergische Halsgerichtsordnung, 1508

[to face p. 30

Nuremberg, has left us an account of the " crimes and evil deeds ", imprisonment and execution of Dr· Nikolaus Gülcher, or von Gülchen, which is preserved in several manuscripts.[2] One of these manuscripts takes the form of a separate pamphlet, with special pagination, inserted in a quarto volume, which was formerly in the possession of the well-known Nuremberg Polyhistor, Christoph Gottlieb von Murr, and is now in the Library of the Germanic Museum, where it bears the reference MS. 3837, 4to. This codex, which seems certainly to date from the first quarter of the eighteenth century, is written in one hand and calls for our special attention, for amongst other things, and although only a copy, it contains the Memorial of a Nuremberg cleric, who for nearly sixteen years, from 1605 to 1620, by direction of the council and in company with Wolfgang Lüder, deacon of St. Sebald's (appointed also to the same office) comforted the condemned criminals with holy words and attended them on their last journey. The detailed record which he has left us of his activities and of his observations and experiences are in many ways and not least from the point of view of psychology, of special importance, and it is only to be regretted that, in spite of all my researches, I have not yet been able to discover the original manuscript.

Nevertheless, the existing copy, although not free from errors, is on the whole good and reliable, as is

[2] See above, p. 22, note 1, in Waldau's *Beyträge*.

shown by a comparison of separate cases cited with the reports of the proceedings in the official records, and also by a comparison of the names. This Memorial offers at the same time the most important additions to the official codifications. In these at times, for one reason or another, the details of a particular case are omitted, a reference being added to the original protocol. Thus, in the record of the trial and execution of the abandoned adulteress Barbara Schlümpfin (MS. 219, fo., Amts-und Standbücher, p. 65b, under date 14 October, 1620, the date of the execution), we find the following :

> N.B. Although it was proposed to write down the various statements made by this same Barbara Schlümpfin while in the Tower and the Loch, as in the case of other malefactors and executed persons, yet other considerations prevailed. Therefore, the records will be found in the Greater Register.

As, however, bundle 219 containing the original proceedings, which is referred to in the margin, has not been preserved, we should be but imperfectly informed concerning the atrocious offences laid to the charge of the delinquent, and her dissolute life, had not the author of the Memorial reported the facts in detail. This is the last execution which he records, and it is interesting less on account of the crimes themselves, which have no particular or social interest, than as a characteristic example of the writer's style. It is printed in Appendix I. The value of this Memorial is also greatly enhanced by the fact that, immediately on his appointment as chaplain, the author obtained permission from the council to have access to the official records, so that he might be correctly informed both concerning the proceedings and the offences which had been committed.

Who then was the cleric to whose careful labours we owe these details which are of such great and varied importance ? Murr himself came to the conclusion that the author was Magister Georg Müller, deacon of St. Sebald's, founding his belief on the fact that the manuscript contains also a report of the proceedings against Nikolaus Gülcher, the authorship of which, on the strength of a holograph copy, was ascribed by Waldau to this same Magister Müller. Murr noted his conclusions frequently in the margin of the Memorial itself, but to Murr's remarks here and there the words *non quod* have been added in another hand. Moreover, Magister Müller had departed this life a year and a half before the date when the Memorial was concluded. Again, in the official acts and private records, as well as in Müller's report of the case of Gülcher, ' Master Hagendorn ' is repeatedly named as the priest who during the fifteen years in question (1605-1620), together with the cleric Lüder, had charge of the delinquents. There seems therefore to be no doubt that Hagendorn was the compiler of the Memorial.[1]

[1] Dr. Albrecht Keller of Wiesbaden, mentions in his edition of Meister Franz Schmidt's Diary (see p. 23, n. 2), p. xi, that the records of Hagendorn, the chaplain of St. Sebald's, who was charged with comforting the criminals, are still in existence. He was unable, in reply to my letter, to recall the authority for this statement. It is not likely that he had before him the missing original manuscript, but he would

33

Magister Johann Hagendorn was born on 1 October 1563 at Hersbruck. He first attended school in his birthplace, and was later a pupil in the elementary school of St. Sebald at Nuremberg. He studied then in different universities, among them Strasburg and Altdorf, and was from 1590 tutor in the house of the Nuremberg patrician Jaochim Nützel. From 1592 he was inspector of the Alumneum at Altdorf, and from 1596 deacon of St. Sebald's. In 1620 he was chosen to be steward of the Chapter at St. Sebald's, and it was doubtless as a result of this appointment that he was charged with the responsible duty of looking after the spiritual welfare of condemned criminals. In 1623 'Johann Hagendorn, steward at St. Sebald's', appears in the 'Parchment Burgher-Book' of 1620-1664, at the head of the thirty Nuremberg clerics and school-officials, to whom the council of the Imperial city granted the privilege of burghers ('Actum Quarta adi 32 Julii anno 1623'). He died on 29 April 1624 and was laid to rest in St. John's Cemetery. The inscriptions on his gravestone (No. 2061 in the cemetery) : 'It is finished', and 'I live that ye may live', serve to remind us of his earthly pilgrimage, and

appear to have used either Murr's manuscript, which does not name the author of the Memorial, or some other reference to the Hagendorn Opus. Apart from these considerations, it should be noted that the Nuremberg Town Librarian, Georg Wolfgang Karl Lochner, as early as the year 1856, copied the Murr manuscript in extenso, and added a detailed introduction, an appendix on the case of Jeremiah Imhof, and an index (which is unfortunately only chronological), and, doubtless with a view to the publication of the Memorial, indicated on his title page that Magister Johann Hagendorn was its author. I desire to express my thanks for the friendly loan of Lochner's work, with a view to the ultimate publication of the Memorial, to Dr. Ernst Mummenhoff of Nuremberg.

his care for the poorest of the poor and their souls' welfare.[1]

In view of the fact that it is my intention to return at length to the life and works of Magister Johann Hagendorn, in connection with the edition of his Memorial which I am preparing, it is only possible here to refer briefly to the remaining contents of the Murr codex above mentioned, in which a copy of Hagendorn's Memorial is preserved. This codex is superior to many of the other malefactors' books of private origin by reason of a certain critical attempt at precision and completeness, which is, however, not always successful. Indeed, certain extracts at the end of the sixteenth century, and again in the middle of the seventeenth century, give one the impression, from their wealth of detail, that the writer was drawing on sources other than the private records which are known to us. Moreover, for the period 1501-1524 the compiler speaks of a book 'in the possession of the barefooted monks in this place' as his original. It is clear, therefore, that he was at some trouble to obtain trustworthy information.

The division of the volume is so contrived that the main bulk of it (283 pages) is concerned with malefactors who were either executed or reprieved after sentence of death in Nuremberg from 1298 to 1723. A smaller

[1] Compare with this summary concerning Johann Hagendorn, Will=Nopitzsch, *Nürnbergisches Gelehrten-Lexikon*, vol. II (1756), p. 12; Joh. Martin Trechsels, *Erneurtes Gedächtnis des Nürnbergischen Johannis-Kirch-Hofs* (1735), pp. 156f. *Amts=und Standbücher*, Nuremberg State Archives, MS, 301, fo. (das pergamentene Bürgerbuch), fo. 5.

division, separately paged, follows (pp. 1-12) concerning ' Malefactors in Nuremberg from 1382-1689 who were begged free ' (freigebeten) ; then follow (pp. 12-50), ' the persons who suffered bodily punishments ' ; and finally (pp. 51-56), ' the persons who came out of prison ', i.e. prison-breakers, a subject which is treated more or less in detail.

In concluding this survey, which is intended to offer a selection only from the vast mass of relevant manuscript material used in the preparation of this work, we must notice finally an equally important source which takes its place mid-way between the two characteristic groups of private records above mentioned. This is the manuscript No. 226 of the Amts-und Standbücher [Registers of offices and rank] in the Nuremberg State Archives : ' Judgments and Executions upon Malefactors from the year of Christ 1600 to this present year 1692, gathered together by Georg Frommoder, Not. Caes. Publ.'

In this folio volume, which is written in a uniform and beautiful script, the Imperial public notary Frommoder has, for the period covered, followed the actual wording of the death sentences (malefactors judgments), or Urgichten, taken doubtless from the official acts to which he could easily obtain access, but he writes the word Urgicht at times Uhrgericht, which shows that its meaning was no longer understood. He adds also many details concerning the actual executions from his own observations and experience, and, like

Magister Johann Hagendorn, he is well informed as to the course of the proceedings, the particulars of which he may well have obtained by inspection of the entries in the Halsgerichts-or Urgichtbücher. Thus he supplies many details concerning the crimes and death by burning (15 November, 1659) of the shepherd boy Hans Rappold of Ansbach, a youth of fifteen or sixteen years, who had abandoned himself to the practice of sodomy, and of whose misdeeds the official manuscript (No. 224, folios 75b-76a) makes no mention. He adds also, at times, particulars concerning malefactors in other places and their 'justification' (at Prague, Bayreuth, Breslau, and other places), and his description of the execution of a wholesale murderer at Breslau in 1654, at which Frommoder tells us he was present, is given in Appendix II as an example of his style and diction.

For the rest we must return to our main subject, the actual contributions which our sources offer for this study of social history—the criminal aspect of the matter has already been sufficiently exploited and studied. We must try to picture the world of crime of the past centuries, and then the life of the burgesses, including in our survey the hangman and his assistants, and see how these two opposing forces are presented to us by the various malefactors' registers. Where it has been necessary or desirable to refer to particular acts and codices I have adopted the following abbreviations:

A. signifies ' Achtbücher '[1] (MSS. 209-220 of the Amts-und Standbücher [Registers of offices and rank] in the State Archives at Nuremberg).

F. George Frommoder's ' Elaborat ' (MS. 226, folio, of the State Archives).

H. Magister Johann Hagendorn's ' Memorial '.

M. refers to the remaining contents of the manuscript formerly in the possession of Murr : and

U. to the Urgicht-or Halsgerichtsbücher[1] (MSS. 221-225 in the Nuremberg State Archives).

---

[1] [I have not attempted to render into English the titles of the official records referred to by Dr. Hampe, but the following note may help to explain the character of the two principal registers.

The *Urgichts-or Halsgerichtsbücher* contain the statements made by the prisoners, the confessions obtained under torture, and the texts of the judgments.

The *Achtbücher*, at first containing the registers of banishments in cases where sentence of death was either not pronounced or not carried out, were used later to record the official proceedings, or protocols, on which judgment was finally pronounced.]

Chapter I

THIEVES OF ALL KINDS

By far the greatest amount of space in the official records is occupied by those crimes and offences which are included under the heading of thefts. The cause lies in the general disposition to seize other people's goods, which in times of economic necessity was often accompanied with violence, and this although, even after the introduction in 1532 of Charles V's criminal code known as the 'Carolina', which modified the awful rigours of the old medieval legal system, the crime was still punished with the utmost severity. In cases, both before and after 1532, where the value of the stolen goods or wares exceeded a gulden, the penalty was death. In addition it must be remembered, in connection with this enactment, that in cases of theft the proceedings and investigations were continued almost without end, until under torture and mental torment every crime has been rehearsed, and each stolen article set down in the protocol. These enquiries as a rule occupy very many folios in the Achtbücher. So, in consonance with the underlying principles of the Carolina, which demanded the clearest

insight into evil-doing, and a corresponding and appropriate punishment, the same course was adopted with debauched persons, and particularly with loose women charged with the capital offence of adultery. These creatures were forced by every means to disclose the names of all persons with whom in the course of their whole lives they had had sinful dealings, to count them up one by one, and in each case to enumerate the number of transgressions.

There is on the whole in such matters little of interest objectively or even from the point of view of social history. Nevertheless something of value may emerge, even here, for the study of language, nomenclature and local history and the records contain a good deal besides which is curious and noteworthy. Although questions such as these are outside our scope, I have assembled in Appendix III the names of certain thieves and robbers in the sixteenth century, while in Appendix IV I have collected a list of the Nuremberg inns which are mentioned in our official records.

I turn now to the variety of trades and types which we encounter in these records. It is amazing to learn from the reports of the examinations the extent to which many of these thieves had roamed about the world before they met their fate at Nuremberg. The cut-purses or pick-pockets were naturally attracted above all to localities and assemblies where, by reason of the crowds of people, they could ply their trade more easily. The Imperial Diets, the fairs, the fencing schools which increased greatly during the sixteenth century, and gatherings such as these offered many opportunities. An example of the career of an incorrigible rogue of this type is provided by an extract from the confessions of one Hans Meller or Moler, ' called Reuter-Henslein, a thatcher and burgher of Gostenhof ', who was arrested for swindling, card-sharping and bigamy (more correctly trigamy, for he had three women on his conscience), and hanged by Master Franz on 18 February, 1585.[1] The extract is from the appropriate Achtbüch (MS. 210).

His associates are given at the commencement as ' the Melchior, and the fair Annalein '. Hans, among other knaveries, ' steeped yellow turnips in fat, stuck hair on to them ' and sold them fraudulently as mandrakes. This he denied until he was confronted by a witness who deposed as to the fraudulent mandrakes.

> ' Then this rascally fellow offered freely to disclose all his thefts, and admitted that it was two years since he commenced his frauds and villainies (fo. 176b), that he has perfected himself therein and practised them to the best of his ability.
>
> Firstly, he practised with cards such cunning that he gave to those with whom he played three kings and a knave. As against this he retained the king of hearts, and in addition three of the same suit, and thus won the game. . . .
>
> (Fo. 177a) And since matters had gone so far, he was forced to confess that, when he was not playing, he stole and took whatever he found.

[1] Ed. Albrecht Keller, p. 17.

And, firstly, Henslein of Lautenhofen, called also the Bavarian Henslein, had cut from the sleeve of a merchant's servant and taken 30 gulden at the fencing-school at Frankfurt during a crush of people and that his share had amounted to 10 gulden . . . (a theft in the market-place at Kitzingen follows).

At Würzburg, during a market, he and Bavarian Henslein's wife had committed knavery with a fire-lock maker or dealer, in that Bavarian Henslein's wife stole from the aforesaid fire-lock maker a pair of fine new gauntlets which she sold at Lengenfeld (Langenfeld) for 4 gulden. . . . In the foregoing summer, at the fencing-school here, he stole a cap which he pledged and pawned to Mathias, the Jew at Fürth for 5 gulden etc. (Then follow thefts at Bamberg, at a country-estate called Kaupershof, at Iphofen and Neumarkt.)

At Augsburg, at the last Imperial Diet, he was present with Hans Hofmann, formerly a gunner here (fo. 178a), and his two brothers Thomas Hofmann and Flöepeutel (thieves' name : ? fly-purse), and had committed thefts there ; that when the Emperor was trumpeted to table, the said Thomas Hofmann, in the press of people, had stolen from the breeches, or trunk-hose, of a noble gentleman, an Imperial councillor, 26 pieces of gold, among which were some worth 24 Batzen [roughly 24 pence] and one worth 10 or 12 gulden. Of these not more than 4 pieces, each worth 24 Batzen, fell to his share, and they all then remained at Augsburg until the Diet was ended '. (Then follow further thefts at Bamberg, Forschheim, Mainz, Neusess, at the Frankfurt fair, as well as in the town of Schwarzach, together with the details of his three alleged marriages.)

We have particulars also of a very shrewd individual in the person of ' Gabriel Wolff, the surviving son of the deceased Hans Wolff, otherwise Glaser, burgher and illuminator of this town ', who as a boy received instruction from the well-known writing and arithmetic master Stephan Brechtel the elder (A.), and who on

11 October 1593 was executed with the sword and then burnt. A detailed account of his frauds, embezzlements, and thefts in all countries can be read in Master Franz Schmidt's Diary (ed. Keller, p. 36). The appropriate Achtbuch indicates as the chief centres of his activities Lisbon, Constantinople, Malta, Venice, Candia (Crete), Lübeck, Hamburg, Messina, Prague, Vienna, Ratisbon, Niederaltaich, Cracow, Danzig, Copenhagen, Stettin, Leipzig, London and so on ; all of which are mentioned in the official examination as to his misdeeds.

So, for instance, with the gingerbread makers' apprentice and fencer Georg Praun (compare Meister Franz, p. 57f). of whom among other things, it is reported that he learnt the gingerbread trade from his father Simon Praun of Mannsfeld, then with a certain Master Jann in Copenhagen ('but there is no one so-called in that place'), from whom he stole 4 gulden's worth of gingerbread. He then continued his appreticeship with a master in Posen and in various other places. ' And should he only receive pardon on this occasion ', so runs the conclusion of the examination (in A.), ' he will take it for a warning throughout his whole life, and betake himself to a country where is known neither to man nor beast. He begs for grace '. But justice had to take its course, and on 14 September 1602 he was executed with the sword.

It would appear from what has been related concerning the Bavarian Henslein, and his association with the

THE HANGMAN'S BRIDGE, NUREMBERG
From a drawing in the Town Library

[to face p. 44

delinquent Hans Meller, that we can trace some kind
of organization of the trade of thieving at the close of
the sixteenth century. Several reports seem also at
times to indicate a regular education in stealing and
purse-cutting. Of one, Stephan Rebeller, who was
executed on 21 June, 1593 (Meister Franz, p. 33f),
it is reported that he kept boys to cut purses and gave
them for their labours each week a thaler and expenses,
together with free board and lodging. He denied
during the enquiry that he had instructed them
(A., M.S. 211, fo. 213a ; M. II, 88), which in itself
provides evidence that training such as this existed,
and on 22 December 1677 ' a single man, who had
begged with forged letters and taught four boys how
to remove money secretly from people's pockets, was
exposed in the pillory, and he and the four boys were
banished from the town ' (M., II, 47).

We hear also of all manner of thieving implements,
spits, fire-locks, bundles of keys, crooked nails, and what
not. And once, in the case of the housebreaker Paulus
Kraus (1616, compare Meister Franz, p. 79), who was
a source of danger to all the summer houses in the
neighbourhood of the town, a very refined kind of
instrument is mentioned, ' a drill which had a cutting-
iron beside the bit to cut the wood in boring, so that
a man's hand could be inserted ' (M., I, 216).

In the case of insignificant or isolated offences
against property the penalty was mostly whipping with
rods, or some other severe and shameful punishment.

45

Thus, in 1581, a butcher's girl charged with thefts of all kinds had to carry the stone round the market place; 'she was the last female who carried the stone'[1] (M., II, 23). On 19 January 1587 'Heinrich Zizmann of Heuchling (close to Lauf), a thief, who declared that he had been to the Venusberg, and knew where the treasure was buried, and stated further that the devil had twice given him money by the stone bridge above Lauf (which was untrue, for he had stolen it elsewhere), was whipped out the town with rods' (M., II, 29). Again, on 18 February 1615, 'the local *s(it) v(enia)* dogkiller', for numerous thefts and attempt at house-breaking, was whipped out of the town and banished (F.).

In general, however, backsliding thieves were punished with all the rigours of the law, and refinements were permitted which strike us as grotesque, if not inhuman. In 1497 'Elizabeth, daughter of Schellen-Claus, a notable thief, was apprehended on account of her thefts, and later buried alive beneath the gallows. This poor creature struggled until the skin on her hands and feet was so lacerated that the people greatly pitied her. Therefore your honourable council was moved to direct that thereafter no female should be buried alive, but that they should be drowned, and

---

[1] [This was the punishment reserved exclusively for women. They were paraded through the streets with great stones fastened round their necks or tied to their feet. Two such stones may still be seen hanging outside the Town Hall at Damme, near Bruges. See M. Letts, *Bruges and its Past*, second ed., 1926, p. 76. Wyclif refers to the punishment in a sermon as a London custom then in disuse. Workman, *John Wyclif*, Oxford, 1926, vol. II, p. 219.]

thereafter such as had stolen either lost their ears or were drowned ' (M., I, 21).

The drowning of women guilty of child-murder took place on the Hallerwiese.[1] At times the Achtbücher have in the margin beside the text a note by the learned clerk to the council: ' submersa pegneso '. At the commencement of the eightieth year of the sixteenth century the sentence on infanticides was changed from drowning to death by the sword, and for women thieves, as well as for their male associates, the punishment was hanging, although in most cases the favour of the sword was granted.

A further privilege is met with in exceptional cases, when, for instance, a delinquent was able to find a respected or influential patron. This will be dealt with at greater length in a later chapter. As a rule, however, pleas of this kind, which were frequently put forward, had little or no effect.

On 15 March, 1610, Hans Mayer ' the son of the deceased Christoph Mayer, cloth dresser, of this town ' was brought to judgment for thefts which to our idea seem insignificant enough. The details can be read in Master Franz's Diary (p. 69), where he is called Körnmayer (the proceedings are absent from the Achtbuch). Magister Hagendorn tells us that he was given the nickname of cock-man,

' because in the days of his apprenticeship, while he was learning the trade of compass-making, he always wore cocks'

[1] [The Hallerwiese formed a promenade for the citizens outside the existing Haller Gate.]

feathers in his hat, whence he acquired the name. He was about twenty years old, a brisk young fellow, so that the girls in the Loch [prison] all fell in love with him, each one more than the other, and if they had not been restrained they might have had more than they bargained for. . . . But since there was no hope of his improvement, judgment was given that he should be hanged until he was dead. He was, however, granted the favour of the sword on account of his youth and the extraordinary pleas which had been put forward, for not only had his mother and her five children interceded for him, of which children two were of the same parentage, and three were of the half-blood, but petitions has also been lodged by his own master, the Rinder, and the whole fraternity of compass-makers. Upon this he maintained his former bearing, and was content to die " right chivalrously ".'

This deliverance from the shameful rope, and the substitution of the more honourable, or less dishonourable, sword, aroused at times feelings of such extravagant gratitude on the part of the wretched criminals that it is difficult for us to understand them. A few examples will suffice. When the thieves Hans Ulrich and Benedikt Felbinger (compare Meister Franz, p. 74) received, at the hands of Magister Hagendorn

' the joyful news that they had been granted this favour, they both fell upon their knees, lifted up their hands, and gave thanks to God and the magistracy. After this they showed their gratitude to us (Magister Hagendorn and Magister Lüder) by kissing our hands. Summa : they did not know what to do or say for joy. And when they had been sentenced to death (with the sword) they thanked the magistrates for their gracious judgment, and when they were carried out they blessed the people and begged for forgiveness and so forth.'

In the same year it is related in the Memorial of

Magister Hagendorn, of the purse-cutter Hans Dietz of Frankfurt, 'called otherwise Frankfurt Hänslein' (compare Meister Franz, p. 74f), that he was at last prepared to die,

> 'if only he could obtain favour with the magistracy and be executed with the sword. When I brought him the good news that a favourable judgment would be given, he was so delighted and comforted that he kissed the hands of both of us, and also the goaler's, and most diligently thanked us. Before the court, during the reading of the judgment he wept bitterly, and returned thanks for the merciful sentence. On his way out he sang almost continuously, so that the people, and even the executioner himself, were moved to pity '.

Among other curiosities it may be mentioned here that the thief and verse-maker Anna Maria Heftrich, who was beheaded, with her sons Hans Peter Heftrich, in 14 November 1719, wrote some verses while she was in the Loch. These have been preserved for us by the unknown compiler of Murr's manuscript, and are not without a certain popular talent. They are dedicated to the head-gaoler, who is referred to as the Host of the Green Frog[1] :

> 'This is my song to the host of the Loch.
> My brothers, do not seek his hospitality.
> He will consume your lives and honour ;
> Never shall I sojourn there more.
>
> . . . .
>
> Who is it that sings this song ?
> I know her well, yet do not ask ;
> She sang her song and pondered much.
> Farewell, mine host, a thousand good nights.

---

[1] Compare H. Knapp, *Das Lochgefängnis*, p. 14.

It is not a little revolting, especially in view of the date, to find that when the thief Leonhard Körner was hanged on 10 June 1738, his mistress was forced to witness the execution, after which she was taken back again to gaol. But the cruelty and ruthlessness of the old criminal law and procedure will be fully present to us in the succeeding chapters.

The number of experts among thieves in general seems to have been almost as large in the sixteenth and seventeenth centuries as it is to-day. We hear, for instance, in 1613, of a corn thief 'who entered the granaries on the Walch with the help of keys and pick-locks which he had made himself, and stole the corn from the bins, and carried it away in baskets'. His offence was aggravated by the fact that he placed his sister, disguised as a ghost, to watch close to the corn-lofts, 'so that the people, when they saw her, were seized with terror and none would pass that way' (H.). In 1615 the goat-thief Hans Beer, 'called otherwise the fat butcher' (H.), of whom an account is given in chapter IX, hanged himself in prison.

I have dealt elsewhere in detail with the proceedings and the execution of the silver-thief Hans Schrenker of Trossenberg (1609), as reported by Magister Hagendorn.[1] Another expert of the same kind was the jewel thief, Jacob Faber.

'He was 24 or 25 years old, by trade a tailor, but he worked little, having applied himself to stealing at the court

---

[1] Compare Bayerischer Heimschütz, XXI (1925) pp. 55f.

of Würtemberg, and later from the knights and noblemen whom he served, and this not only in Germany, but also in Italy, France, and wherever he journeyed with them. He learnt his business in so masterly a manner, that when he arrived here at the end of 1619, during a conference between the electors and other princes ', he stole from the goldsmith Hans Carpentier ' gold, silver, precious stones and finished articles ' to the value of 2,000 gulden. When he was taken and sentenced to be hanged, the clerics had a difficult time with him. "When I came to him," writes Magister Hagendorn, "he was ready with all his old tricks. He urged his honourable friendships, particularly the claims of his old and helpless mother, and put forward all manner of excuses why he should continue to live and escape the death penalty. He cared more for his body than his soul, and as he was troublesome before the council, so with us, not indeed in the matter of instruction and comfort, for he had studied and learnt the catechism in his tender youth, and knew certain psalms likewise, particularly the 6th and 23rd, with other prayers, but by his obstinate adherence to his old ways. Whether we told him sweet or bitter things, his only purpose was to go on living ".'

A very different picture is presented in the story of the thefts and conduct of Hans Übelhack, ' burgher and watchmen of the Spittler Gate in this town ', who was at last successfully interceded for, so that his case does not figure in the official Achtbuch. He had stolen from Master Paulus Beheim

' while he was master of the dungeon at the Spittler Gate, a copper hanging cauldron, together with certain pewter plates and glasses, all of which he had pledged with a Jew at Fürth. Finally, when Master Georg Volckamer, who took over the said prison after Master Paulus Beheim, wished to give a banquet there, on a Wednesday, the day on which there was cock-chasing[1] at Gostenhof (but it was abandoned

[1] It is not known what popular merrymaking is here referred to.

on account of the rain), he stole 3 fine tablecloths, of which one was valued at 5 florins, certain napkins, 6 spoons, with silver bowls, as well as copper and pewter utensils, four times as much as he could carry in his arms. These he hid in the lattice-work, omitting to mention that he had counterfeit keys, and could come down from the tower when he liked. Then it was adjudged, and sentence was given, that he should be hanged until he was dead. On account, however of the prayers of his old and helpless wife (he was himself only 37 years old), and of certain neighbours, and specially on the part of two elderly gentlemen whom he had robbed, and seeing that Master Volckamer had had his goods again, his life was spared, and on the following Friday (21 August 1618), together with a lusty peasant, he was whipped out of the town. . . . He would as lief have left his head behind him as be whipped, as he told us several times, and later, when he had taken the oath of reconciliation, he is said to have repeated the statement '.

A story is also told of a post-bag thief 'formerly the courier of Altdorf', who four days before he was to be hanged (1617) was seized with a violent fever, 'which he carried with him to the gallows', as Magister Hagendorn tells us rather brutally, 'and from which he was not recovered until Master Franz hanged a cure about his neck'. In 1617, and again in 1676 we meet with thieves who stole bronze from the epitaphs in the Nuremberg cemeteries. In one of these cases (1617) the criminals were the 'ear-ring maker' Hans Mager, and the goldsmith Casper Lenker, both Nuremberg burghers. They were left long in anguish and fear of death, but finally they were pardoned on the intercession of the goldsmiths' craft and many friends and kinsmen. In addition a cousin of Caspar Lenker of

Augsburg ' who is the leading goldsmith there ' (H.)—
this seems to have been the distinguished master of his
craft, Johannes Lenker (d. 1637)—made special
supplication, as did finally ' an emissary from Lorraine '
who chanced just then to be in Nuremberg.

When in 1541 the Beautiful Fountain in the Market
place was restored and re-gilded ' a low fellow was
taken at night as he was preparing to scrape off the
gold ', for which offence he was whipped out of the
town.

Poachers appear from time to time, as well as gipsies,
who with their thefts and robberies and murderous
attacks had become by the commencement of the
eighteenth century, a veritable terror to the country-
side. I propose to deal with the executions of gipsy-
women in 1733 in greater detail in the ' Einkehr '
supplement to the Münchener Neueste Nachrichten,
but I will notice here in passing two more representa-
tives from among the light-fingered community in
old Nuremberg. In the case of Wolf Brezenstengel
(1612), we are introduced to a regular cat-burglar,
whose masterpiece was a climb to a the third storey of a
house, ' but this was his undoing and prevented him
from obtaining the favour of the sword ', although the
whole stonemasons' craft, to which he belonged, as
well as his three sisters and his unhappy mother, all
interposed on his behalf. The sisters indeed fell on
their knees before the Treasurer, Master Paulus
Harsdörfer, and Master Pfinzing. ' But in vain. The

magistrates allowed it to be spread abroad that since he was such a master of climbing, he had better practice his art on the ladder ' (of the gallows) (H.).

As an example of the manners of the ' good old times ' we may mention the gallows-thieves, who appear from time to time in our official records without any indication that they were followed or captured. Thus Matthes Lenzer (as it appears from A.) ' cooper and burgher here, a traitor and thief', who was hanged on 15 June 1591, was robbed in the following night of all his clothes down to his stockings, ' so that it was necessary to dress him in a shirt and trunk-hose ' (M.) ; while on 23 April 1642, the heads of two women child-murderers, which in accordance with the practice had been set up as a warning on the scaffold, were removed from the Rabenstein, doubtless for superstitious purposes. ' He who did this is a proper gallows-thief ' (M.).

In concluding these extracts concerning the thieves of the Imperial city of Nuremberg, it may be fitting to give (from Magister Hagendorn's Memorial) some particulars of the last hours of the thief Georg Merz of Gibitzenhof, called otherwise ' der Schlegel ' (the mallet). He was a young, lusty peasant of about twenty-two years, and the description of his journey to the place of execution is exceedingly grotesque.[1] Already in prison he had behaved himself so foolishly

---

[1] For further particulars see Frommoder's description of the same scene at the end of Chapter X of this book.

and capriciously that the woman-gaoler had likened him
to Marcolphus of the twelfth century minstrel poem
' Salman und Morolf ', whose long life showed much the
same characteristics.   He insisted on being carried out
and executed in his black cap and woollen shirt.

> ' He begged me ', writes Magister Hagendorn, ' for the
> love of God to let him have his way with the cap, as he
> would then do all that was required of him.   I should see
> with what gaiety, resignation and despatch, as he said, he
> would then go forth.   And in truth he went out hastily,
> for as soon as he has left the Loch immediately his *spiritus
> ebrietatis vel vertiginis* seized him, and he began to yell and
> to play the fool.   " Mine is the day, be comforted, dear
> people ", he cried out, with much else, and three times I
> had to return and help to drive him along.   When we
> reached the Hall (i.e. the Court), he repeated the same words
> with loud cries, so that I had to restrain him and admonish
> him to be more moderate.   Before the court he exhibited
> himself, grinning like an idiot, turning first to the right, then
> to the left, fleshing his teeth, and twisting his mouth so that
> I had twice to correct and admonish him. . . .   When
> he was sentenced he bowed himself, as if to show reverence
> to the council, and almost fell in a heap.   When we came
> down with him from the Rathaus we could scarcely control
> him.   He leapt in the air, raged, and fumed, as if he were
> raving mad. . . .   Then he gave orders that they should
> bring the chair, and when he had seated himself, and was
> bound, he began to stamp with his feet like a horse, raising
> and dropping his head, exulting and crying out :   " I am
> comforted : my faith has saved me ".   He called the people
> angels, and many times requested that his hat might be
> removed so that he could see the angels.   ' He continued
> his half-crazy tricks without intermission the whole way to
> the gallows, so that the chair on which he sat was over-
> turned.   As we came close to the execution place I showed
> him the gallows, hoping that the sight would quieten him.
> But he answered me that he was already dead, and cried out

to the gallows, " Be comforted my brothers, I am coming ".
. . . When he had asked the people to pardon from the place of execution, and had prayed, finishing with the Pater Noster, I asked him in a loud voice to whom he would commend his soul, since he was about to die. Whereat he laughed aloud and cried out : " How now soul " ! which gave me such pain that I could not speak another word to him. As he spoke the words ' God the Father be with us and save us from destruction ', I repeated them with him, until the rope was placed round his neck. I then asked him in whose name he was going to die, and he cried out, ' In Christ's '. Then I repeated with him the text, ' Lord, into thy hands I commend my spirit ', but before it was finished he had been thrown off the ladder. God have mercy on his soul and forgive those who had misled him. I did my duty by him faithfully, both in the Loch and while he was being carried out, but did not speak much with him, as I saw that he threw all my heartfelt admonitions to the winds, and frequently turned them to laughter, and I remembered that one should not throw holy things to the dogs, nor cast pearls before swine. But Magister Lüder spoke more with him, and was not to be put down in his efforts. Magister Christoph Reich made the following epitaph for him :

> Fur suspendendus voces jactabat inanes
> Atque atras furcas ibat ovans animis ;
> Verum ubi quadrantem miser ille pependerat horae
> Amplius haud verbum '.

In English so :

The thief must be hanged : he cries aloud in his folly ;
And climbs to the gallows, his heart exulting within him.
But the wretch, having hung for a space,
Nevermore did he open his lips.

Chapter II

VIOLENCE, PLUNDER AND INCENDIARISM, MURDER AND HOMICIDE

It is often difficult to say how far we can credit the information contained in unofficial compilations, unless the author was a man of authority or an eyewitness. As an example of this I will commence the present chapter with a notice from the Murr manuscript for the year 1505 :

'On Wednesday, SS. Simon and Judas Day (22 October), it runs, 'Georg Graffen, a sturdy pouch-maker, for various crimes, had his eyes put out '.

It is clear that this entry relates to the blind Landsknecht and poet Jörg Graff, whose wild and adventurous life, as presented in his poems and in the comparatively rich manuscript material in our archives, I attempted to relate some twenty years ago[1]. His fate formed also the subject of the delightful story by the Austrian poet, Franz Karl Ginzkey, *Der Wiesenzaun*.

The early date must in itself arouse suspicion, for the poet, according to the documents, is not to be found in Nuremberg until 1517, and it is only in 1518 that the chronicles report the burning of the White Tower which he atoned for with his eyes. On the other hand, he is already reported to be blind in 1517, and it is therefore possible that the date in the Malefactors' Book, although surprising, should be accepted as against the entry in the chronicles. As he is described in the manuscript as a sturdy pouch-maker [Beutler]—the word sturdy signifying something disreputable—it is possible that Beutler should read Bettler[beggar]. This suggests that he was a cut-purse, but, if so, it seems certainly to be a mistake. It arose possibly from the fact that Jörg Graff belonged to the pouch-makers' craft before he became a Landsknecht, and that his name was accidentally set down in the official records with the addition of pouch-maker. In 1529, after he had slain a man and had been banished,

---

[1] See Euphorion, VI (1897), pp. 457ff, and, in extended form, in the Supplement to the Allgemeine Zeitung, 1898, Nr. 217 (17 September).

and had gradually gone from bad to worse, it was the pouch-makers' craft which petitioned the Nuremberg council on his behalf. It is, therefore, not apparent for what crime he can have been blinded in 1505, although a reference may possibly be intended to his subsequent misdeeds. In any event, in view of this notice, the principal events in Jorg Graff's life may have to be critically re-examined.

That the poet was subsequently treated with considerable indulgence was due doubtless to his remarkable popularity. Wilibald Pirckheimer assisted him at times, and obtained for him protection against pirated copies of his poems.

Nevertheless, the punishments for serious crimes, especially before the introduction of the Carolina, were relentless in their severity, and of a dreadful nature. In 1392, it is reported of a cloth maker of Wöhrd (close to Nuremberg), who violated his own mother and then strangled her, that he was boiled in oil. In 1497, according to Murr's manuscript, ' 18 jews, who had murdered four Christian boys in their cellars—a crime which was disclosed by a Jewish girl—were here burnt alive on the Jew's Hill (the present Marfeld) outside the Laufer Gate '.

Even after 1532 the punishments for criminal assaults were often sufficiently severe. In 1562, a leper, one of the ' incurables ', who were as a rule required to live in separate houses and establishments, took occasion, during the Easter feast in the Neuer

Bau, the present Maximilian-platz, to roam at large, and to embrace ' a neat and beautiful woman called " the Kleeweinin " ; to draw her to him, to press her to his heart and to kiss her ' so that it was necessary to drag her away from him, and to come to her assistance with medicines before she could be restored. Thereupon this ne'er-do-well was executed with the sword ' (M.).

As against this we have a record of three soldiers ' who suffered judgment as malefactors in the Neuer Bau ' for striking the mayor (Schultheiss) and were merely declared to be common rogues and to be dishonourable. A month later another soldier was sentenced to death for bigamy, but upon the intercession of his first wife and 16 other women, he was finally let off with a whipping. For assaults, after 1571, the delinquents were not infrequently sent to the galleys. The daughter of a cobbler who, in the presence of the court, struck a cobbler's apprentice in the neck for having stated that he had slept with her 100 times ' because she could not suffer such a thing ', was paraded by two town officials round the Beautiful Fountain, wearing the fiddle about her neck with her two hands fastened therein, and the slanderous accuser was banished from the town. This carrying of the fiddle is mentioned here and there in eighteenth century records[1].

[1] [The Geige or fiddle was a kind of wooden collar fastened about the neck in which the hands were also locked. There is an illustration in F. R. Heinemann, *Der Richter*, Jena, 1900, illust. No. 118.]

In considering now the various crimes associated with robbery and violence, we must glance for a moment at the robber-knights and freebooters of the old school, who could maintain feuds even with the Imperial city itself, and among whom Eppelein of Geilingen[1] in the fourteenth century, and Hans Schüttensamen in the fifteenth century, are the best known. In connection with the latter, it is characteristic of what we might call the probity of the Nuremberg council that Schüttensamen's servant, who had betrayed his master for the sake of the 600 gulden set upon his head, was ordered, after payment of the blood-money, ' to withdraw himself by sunlight (that is before sunset) from the town of Nuremberg '.

The last of these noble peace-breakers to be beheaded with this band in Nuremberg was Christoph Hessel von Grumbach. When captured he had offered, without avail, 17,000 gulden and one of his castles as the price of his freedom, and after judgment had been pronounced, he twice begged for mercy on his knees. But nothing could save him. The only favour accorded to him was that on his way to the execution place he was absolved from having to wear the common malefactor's cloak, and that the execution took place on a widely-spread black cloth. ' He was buried in the little Church of St. Peter ' (M.).

The Nuremberg council of patricians proceeded

---

[1] [The Götz von Berlichingen of the period. The story of his leap on his favourite horse from the castle walls is familiar to every visitor into Nuremberg. See below, p. 144.]

with equal severity and relentlessness against its own members and colleagues if they were guilty of embezzlement or other misdeeds. In these cases the executions were conducted with added solemnity, and wide publicity was avoided by carrying out the sentence, not at the place of execution outside the Frauentor, but in some other place, specially appointed. In the case of the young patrician Paulus Deichsler, who, in 1565, so sorely wounded two coachmen that one died of his wounds, it was of no avail that numbers of princes and lords pleaded for him. Since the widow of the dead man was not to be appeased, the law had to take its course.

Many degrees below the highly-placed freebooters above mentioned come the hosts of common land-sharks and marauders, the highwaymen and brigands, to whom murder and man-slaying were of small account, and whose depredations tended to increase in times of unrest, particularly in the years following the great wars. A few examples have been collected from Nuremberg's past.

The transition from one group to the other may be noted in the case of Andreas Kessler, a butcher of Dinkelsbühl, who 'denounced'—that is declared a feud against—Count Johann Friedrich zu Öttingen and caused enormous damage by fire and pillage. On 19 November 1551 he was burnt alive as an incendiary. He left a widow and eight children, and the woman was carrying her ninth child. His

beliefs were singular, but he died a Christian' (M.).
' He is a black lean fellow, about fifty years of age '(U).

During the Margrave's war (1553) the robber
Hans Neydel could not be executed at the Rabenstein
outside the town, but like the soldiers mentioned
previously he suffered ' at the Neuer Bau opposite
the Foundling-home,' where a stage or scaffold was
set up (M). Horrible, as were all deaths with the
wheel, was the execution on 4 August 1612 of the robber
Matthäus Werthfritz of Fürth. He was in his 25th or
26th year, small in stature, but very courageous, and
was called "Eight Fingers" because the two first fingers
on the left hand had been shot off before Gran in
Hungary '. He served also in other campaigns, and
fought with great courage against the ' Turkish
hereditary enemies '. His offence was made more
serious by an attempted suicide in prison. He gave
himself

> ' three cuts in the body with an instrument which he had
> concealed, the third penetrated, but not mortally. He
> showed great fortitude up to the moment of his death and
> watched it approach with unfaltering gaze, carrying himself
> the while like a Christian knight. I hope, therefore, that
> through his protracted sufferings and the breaking of his
> limbs he attained to everlasting life. He received 21 blows,
> the first 2 on the neck, then 6 or 8 over the heart, and finally
> his 4 limbs were broken. May God grant him a happy
> resurrection ' (H.).

A touch of humour, however, is provided in the
account by Frommoder of the execution of two foot-
pads and highwaymen, Hans Schwarz of Hanau and

Hans Neuburger of Lübeck, who were beheaded on
4 May 1664.

> ' Nota : As these two victims were laid on the wheel and
> began to rot a great collection of fine gold and silver coins
> fell out, which they had sewn up in their clothes. A butcher's
> boy, who was minding sheep thereabouts, found a great
> many which he kept.'

This record seems to show that the searching of
prisoners in Nuremberg at that time was not done very
thoroughly.

On 22 March 1712 an incendiary named Lorenz
Korber was executed as a favour with the sword, notwithstanding the fact that by law and statute he should
have been burnt alive, but on 20 August 1743 a
highwayman named Johann Michael Fischer, who
robbed in the grand manner, 'was done to death by
breaking of his limbs with the wheel' (A.). A similar
fate overtook the fourfold murderer Michael Gemperlein in 1612, after he had been four times pinched with
red hot tongs. Like Matthäus Werthfritz, in the
same year, he attempted suicide in prison by trying to
hang himself with his night-cap which he had un-
ravelled, but the single threads were not strong
enough. It was only on account of his penitent
confession that finally, as Magister Hagendorn tells us

> ' Our merciful authorities were pleased to show favour and
> to direct the executioner to strike at once over the heart,
> and so to put an end to his life before he broke his limbs.
> This the dying criminal acknowledged, uttering these words :
> he must in truth confess that he had gracious judges '.

The parricide Samuel Bossecker on 10 July 1649 'was broken on the wheel with 22½ blows' (F.).

[A paragraph is here omitted. It can be found at p. 28 of the German edition. It concerns a brutal assault upon a child-bearing woman.]

I propose to deal elsewhere with the psychological and other aspects of the interesting and instructive case of Taucher, which relates to the murder of a poor young waiter, and the theft of the till by a very intelligent youth of eighteen years, with which the official records are much concerned in 1579. I hope likewise to study in detail the murder in 1616 of the 'blue virgin', e.g. Ursula von Ploben, the spinster sister of George Paul von Ploben (d. 1625), the last of the family, whose name is still preserved in the Plobenhof and Plobenstrasse at Nuremberg. In this case, which is reported in all its details by Magister Hagendorn, the old superstition concerning the ordeal of the bier makes its appearance. When one of the murderers, a vassal of the lady of Ploben, with the view of allaying suspicion, proposed to present himself on the morning after the deed with the quarter's rent which was due, he was prevented by the old lady's housekeeper, who was herself a guilty party, 'since she was perturbed lest the corpse might begin to sweat (i.e. to bleed) when the murderer entered the house'. He would be well advised, she said, to send his wife. Another particularly detailed affair of the eighteenth century may be briefly mentioned here, an atrocious

65

crime by a band of robbers who in 1708 attacked a number of lonely mills in the country, and extended their depredations to the Bohemian Forest. Here, as an example, is the account of the attack upon the so-called Neissler Mill, in the words of the official record.

On 13 September 1708 Georg Spörl, called otherwise the ' Black One ', was beheaded and his body fastened to the wheel, while his companion Jacob König, known also as Wurst-Gockel, a confirmed robber and murderer, was broken with the wheel. We have in these two without doubt, the leaders of the dreaded band. It was Georg Spörl who

' with seven male companions, among them two with loaded pistols, and two women had by night broken into a mill near Hilpoldstein, called the Lower Neissler Mill. They forced the miller to disclose his buried money, which he did. Then, since they desired more money, they carried the miller to a room, and there with two maids who chanced to be at the mill (whose faces they covered with rags), they tied them up by their hands and feet, binding the miller tightly with cords. One of the men then tortured them with burning splinters, forcing hob-nails under the nails of their hands and feet, while another beat the miller and one of the girls with a stick because they wanted more money ' . . . (U.).

Finally, there should be mentioned in this connection the poisonings and childmurders, as well as homicides, upon sudden impulse and without criminal intent, all of which were much in evidence during the history of Nuremberg as an Imperial city. Poisonings, or would-be poisonings, which were both capital offences, appear nearly always as a result of unhappy marriages or unlawful desires. The details of such offences have little to offer to the student of social history, but the sequel to the execution of Hans Otzmann (22 September 1674), a peasant of Illhofen, is worthy of notice. He had attempted repeatedly to poison his wife with mouse-poison, which the maids mixed with her food, ' but it did her no harm '. He then tried to drown his wife in a well (M.). ' The executioner's assistant collected his blood in earthen pots, and gave it to drink to persons afflicted with epilepsy, or the falling sickness, whereupon they became cured, healthy, and whole ' (F.). ' The blood was still warm, and three peasants, a youth, and a girl drank of it ' (M.).

The proceedings connected with the crime of infanticide present far more uniformity in their details, as they do to-day, than is the case with proceedings relating to poisonings. They are concerned almost entirely with the sudden, blind, and uncomprehended impulse to conceal the evidence of sin, which delivered the unmarried mother almost invariably into the clutches of the hangman. In cases where ' the child, the offspring of dishonour ', as the expression runs in Murr's manuscript, had been deliberately killed, there was little hope of mercy. The following case from the year 1525 is an exception. The Nuremberg executioner being ill, a substitute was obtained from Rothenburg to drown the child-murderess Gertraut Büttnerin of Bamberg, but the substitute begged the woman free and desired to marry her, which was granted. As a rule the only grace accorded was that the victim should die by the sword. And this dispensation aroused such an excess of gratitude on the part of these terrified creatures, tortured by enquiries, and beside themselves with penitence, that it is easy to see that their minds had become unbalanced. A few examples will serve to illustrate this.

In the case of Anna Lennischerin, who was executed on 16 June 1657, it is reported in the official records that when it was announced to her that the privilege of the sword had been granted,

> 'this poor creature returned thanks for the merciful judgment, and affirmed that in return for the grace shown to her, the good God would reward the most noble and learned council with good fortune and perpetual bodily health, and at the same time she took her leave of all present, wishing them a thousand good-nights, and showed herself as ready to die' (U.).

In the same way in the year 1663 in another case of infanticide :

> 'this poor one returned humble thanks to the most noble and learned council for all the benefits and privileges extended to her, and above all for the merciful judgment, hoping that God would reward their most worthy nobilities with continued health, and much well-being of soul and body' (U.).

Finally in 1668

> 'this poor sinner (Margaretha Irnsingerin) humbly thanked the most noble and learned council for this merciful judgment as well as for all the benefits shown to her during a lengthy period, and exhibited up to the time of her death such a

VARIOUS METHODS OF EXECUTION AND PUNISHMENT
From Tengler, Laienspiegel, 1508

[to face p. 68

Christian and pious spirit, and such whole-hearted penitence
for her crime, that many were greatly moved to wonder
thereat. As she was brought to the place of execution at
the Rabenstein, close to the chair, she halted some two paces
away, and made clear the ardour of her piety in the following
words : " Oh, let me pray further ". Immediately upon
this, when she had scarcely uttered these words, the
executioner (Matthes Pergner) cut off her head standing,
and thus acquitted himself honourably in his first attempt
with the sword " (U.).

We cannot help thinking that the proceedings
against these wretched victims was often harsh and
inhuman. A case in point is that of ' one Anna,
daughter of Christoph Emels, burgher and town-
glazier of Amberg ', who was beheaded for child-
murder on 8 February 1614 by Master Franz (Diary,
p. 74). After she had been carried to prison she became
ill, and had to be transferred to the hospital where she
was carefully restored to health,

' for which the Rotenbeck—probably the barber-surgeon—
allowed it to be known in the establishment that he was a
sorry man, for that which he had built up with such care
Master Franz would destroy. Finally she was returned to
prison with her gaoler, the ancient Fazel, but the latter was
so wrought upon by the bad air and the stink of the hospital
that, when he again reached the Loch, he became sick and
soon died '.

She, however, confessed her misdeeds, and justice
took its course (M.). The story of the end of the
ancient Fazel, who was not likely to have been a
sensitive person, throws a somewhat unfavourable light
upon the conditions in hospital at that time.

It is natural that we should be met at times with morbid conditions, hereditary evils, and other physical disorders, which in those days were only imperfectly understood. Such conditions were clearly the work of the devil, and nothing could be modified either in the judgment to be pronounced or in the sentences to be executed. A few examples will suffice. They deal with child-murder in its precise significance, that is in its relation to deliberate homicide, and illustrate the general attitude to crimes of impulse. In the year 1580 we have the story of a forty-four year old peasant woman, Anna Strölin (compare Meister Franz, p. 10), who in the presence of her four other children ' struck her six year old little boy with a hook in an unnatural and murderous fashion ', and attempted also the lives of her other children but had pity on them. ' It was assumed that the evil fiend had thrown her into a melancholy ' (M.). In 1705 and 1710 we find, in rapid succession, two cases, in each of which, for no apparent reason, ' and purely from wicked design ', a female slew a small child—in the second case the victim was the woman's own legitimate child, a baby of sixteen weeks. The butcher's daughter, Christina Forgerin of Bruck (1709) resolved, as the records tell us, ' on account of a slight ', to attack ' the next best child and to take its life '. Later, having killed a nine-year-old girl, she was seized with repentance, terror, and misery, gave herself up and made a full confession, on account of which ' the pinching with red-hot irons, which she had also deserved, was through favour remitted ', and she was merely executed with the sword (U.).

A prey to an unholy lust for child murder (in 1691) was Maria Magdalena Wolffin, the surviving daughter of Hans Wolff, burgher and furrier, and former wedding bidder[1]. Twice, in her attempts to escape from her awful obsession, she determined to commit suicide, and to throw herself from the Hallerwiese into the Pegnitz, but on each occasion she was restrained immediately before the act ' by the thought that she might thereby imperil her soul ' ; until at last a small child fell a victim to the demon which possessed her. The proceedings, and her struggles for her soul, are described in detail in Murr's manuscript.

Passion, recklessness, sudden anger, uncontrollable impulse, play an important part in offences against the lives of a man's fellow-creatures at all times, particularly when quarrels arise during excess or drunkenness. How insignificant may be the causes which lie behind crimes of this nature may be seen from the case of Dominikus Korn, which is from many points of view of considerable importance for the student of social history. Master Franz (p. 15) mentions the matter on 12 May, 1584, unfortunately in a few lines only. On this day he beheaded the before-mentioned Korn, a Landsknecht, and, as we learn from Murr's manuscript,

---

[1] [This was the official who formally invited guests to weddings, christenings and the like. See above, p. 13.]

the son of the host of the Golden Post Horn at Nuremberg, who slew in a quarrel a nobleman and soldier the ensign Ninus von Wixenstein. The scene, which took place in a barber-surgeon's room, is in its beginnings by no means clear. I give the first part literally for purposes of discussion.

'Among other things', says Dominikus Korn, 'the ensign enquired of Hipler (i.e. another Landsknecht called Franz Hippler) what fresh news he had, and where he was stationed. Upon this Hipler replied that he was then at Ponn (Bonn am Rhein), and that he had indeed news, but that he could only sing it. The ensign then asked the speaker (that is the delinquent, who is speaking) to write it down for him. This speaker, however, excused himself on the ground that he wrote with difficulty. Thereupon he (? the speaker) sang it by heart to him (the ensign), and told Hipler to write it down, which was done. In writing it down, however, he omitted two sentences, and this speaker, when he saw this, folded the sheets of paper together and put them in his breeches, and produced a fresh piece of paper so that it might be written down again. Upon which the ensign arose and scolded and abused this speaker, and demanded to know how he dared to take his property. He cursed him this way and that, and said that if he were a Landsknecht he should go out of the door and fight with him. As this speaker went outside he, the ensign, called him in through the window, and said that since he had called him out he had better look to himself. And as they both drew their swords this speaker observed that he (the ensign) had received a wound, which he must still have. Beyond this nothing happened.

It was objected[1]

'The matter is far different from what he has presented'.
. . . It was he who first 'abused and smote' the ensign,

[1] [The actual heading is : " Uf furhalten "=Auf Vorhalten. A literal translation is impossible, but what happened is as follows. The prisoner told his story, then the prison magistrates pointed out the reasons why his story could not be accepted, and if he still persisted he was bound and threatened with torture, and, if necessary tortured.]

and thrust at him through the window. He then called out the ensign, 'demanding to know what kind of an ensign he might be; he was nothing but a worthless priest (Dompfaff), and his honour was so touched that it was a shame and sin to have to fight with such a one'. The speaker then thrust at him through the window on either side. Therefore it were better if he told the truth about the affair.

Bound and Threatened

'He says it is not otherwise than that the ensign desired to know his name, and that of his companion (probably Hipler). The speaker asked what he wished to know concerning his name, and may have added that he might be an ensign, but might also be a priest (Dompfaff) as well', and so on. 'He was however so fuddled that he did not know how he came into the barber's house', etc. (The matter continues to the next page and ends without any application of torture.)

Drunkenness was also the downfall of the French soldier Jacob La Maire of Mantes (25 miles east of Paris), who had taken service for the Imperial city. He slew two peasants who, as he learnt, had most evilly abused two of his companions, they being likewise drunk, and had thrown them from the bridge by the Wöhrder meadows into the Pegnitz. As he knew no German beyond the words 'I thank you, father', which he spoke to the cleric, the French schoolmaster, Samuel Herbst, was brought in as interpreter. The whole story, and the culprit's horror at his deed, which was to turn his thirteen children into fatherless orphans, is reported faithfully and in detail by Magister Hagendorn, although the delinquent's conversion from the Catholic to the Protestant faith may be doubted.

Until then we are told the culprit knew little of the Bible and Christ : *Vide quam bene pascant oves papicolae* (MS. 224, fo. of the Amts-und Standbücher [Registers of office and rank] State Archives, Nuremberg, fo. 2b). On 22 October 1618, undismayed and confident, La Maire went to his death after delivering an excellent address, of course in the French language, to the people, who replied with an unusual acclamation, *Deus sit propitius miserae animae*. With these words the writer of the slightly more detailed report in the Urgicht-bücher closes his account.

Politics seem to have been introduced into the case of the lacemaker Peter Schneider, ' a fine strong man ', who in 1619, while he was drunk, stabbed another of the same trade. He was under suspicion of treachery, and judgment and execution were hastened, or, as the expression runs, ' the bells were jingled for him betimes ', so that ' every kind of intercession might be cut short ' (H.). So with the case of Philipp Knorr, which I have considered briefly elsewhere (Bayerischer Heimschutz XXI), whose fate was obviously affected by political considerations. In any event Magister Hagendorn is of opinion that Knorr, who had the death of his wife on his conscience, might possibly have been pardoned, for his wife begged for him on her death-bed, and he rejoiced in the support of many important persons and soldiers. But the Margrave's people, at the instance of the accused, demanded, on the very day when he was to be executed, that his

74

person together with the dead body of his wife (which had already been buried) should be delivered before sunset on that day at Carlsberg (probably Cadolzburg) since the matter lay within the jurisdiction of the Margrave and not within that of Nuremberg. . . .' The question being one of disputed jurisdiction, the Imperial city decided it without discussion by a *fait accompli*.

The curious instance of homicide which took place in 1615 in the Tetzel chapel, in the church of St. Aegidien, must be dealt with elsewhere. But it may be stated here that among the criminals with whom the foregoing extracts are concerned, persons of all ages are represented, from young people, scarcely removed from childhood, to ancient veterans of both sexes. As Nestor of this company we may mention the gardener Simon Birkner, who murdered 'Eva Hoff-männin, his betrothed, during the night' (M.), and was executed with the sword for his crime on 31 January, 1631. 'This same Simon Birkner', adds Frommoder in a note, 'was 82 years of age'.

CHAPTER III

CONCERNING RIOT, PERJURY AND TREACHERY, DEFAMATION AND BLACKMAIL

IN comparison with the serious crimes which have occupied us hitherto, the remaining classes, each one considered by itself, are comparatively unimportant. Further, the individual offences, committed possibly by the same culprit, often in actual or theoretical opposition (as a jurist might say) with offences of a different nature, may nevertheless be conveniently grouped together unless they separate themselves naturally at the outset.

So it falls out that in considering riot and perjury, as they appear in the Malefactors' Books, we are at once brought into touch with a number of fifteenth- or sixteenth-century freebooters, or with the misdeeds of Peter Schneider, already mentioned. Moreover, half-way between this chapter and the last, appears an extraordinary happening which has come down to us from the year 1482, in which year, 'a horseman of the Margrave', that is not a rebel, but a jealous or discontented individual from a more or less hostile camp, thrust with his spear at the carved stone eagle above the Frauentor and knocked off one of its claws. He was apprehended by the watch and ' later beheaded in the Market-place ', as one who had brought the dignity of the council into contempt (M.).

In the time of the great Peasants' War we are faced with a whole series of insurrections against the peace of the State by reformers and fanatics, whose varied activities, already studied in part, seem to deserve a closer investigation. I single out for the moment the case of the rebel Hans of Nuremberg, ' an esquire of Gostenhof ', and Ulrich Aberhenlein, both of whom were beheaded on 5 July 1524. As regards the first, some examples are given of the mutinous speeches which he had delivered to the people, such as, for instance : ' It signified nothing : the upper classes had lots of the money. It was necessary to threaten

77

and kill them, and if it came to that he was prepared to do his share in killing the rich ' (U.).

In August 1525 the peasant leaders Michel Koberer, a miller of Langenzenn, who had helped the revolted peasants of Neustadt a. d. Aisch to come into their own,—' he died like a Christ merrily and willingly ' (M.)—and Michel Hutter, among others, were hurriedly executed in Nuremberg. On 26 March 1527 the anabaptist and anarchist sectarian Wolfgang Vogel, cleric at Eltersdorf, on account of ' wicked and injurious alliance against all authority which he attempted to destroy ', was shortened by a head, although, adds the clerk to the council in an attempt at humour, ' he was already short enough '. I have already dealt with this case on the 400th anniversary of his death in the ' Frankischer Kurier ', and propose elsewhere to consider it in greater detail. On 17 June 1530 (a further echo of the Peasants' War) the butcher Jobst Sporer, was executed, his offence being ,that he attempted to inflame the populace with outrageous and disturbing speeches. (Compare Bayer. Heimschutz XXI, p. 54.)

A disturber of the peace rather than a rebel was Hans Leykauf, ' the avowed enemy of the Kelschen Pruck ', who was executed with the sword on 14 November 1538 (U.). As against this the details of the evil deeds of the ' mighty book-keeper ' (as he was called) and lampoonist, Sebald Herold, are by no means clear, for he must have had much more to his debit

SCENE IN TORTURE CHAMBER
From a coloured drawing (15th Century), Zentralbibliothek, Zürich

[to face p. 78

than his pasquinades. The council purged themselves of this extremely unpleasant person by sentence of death on 22 January 1572. According to the Urgichtbücher (MS. 222, folio 48b, of the Nuremberg State Archives),

> ' he was beheaded (as a favour) because so much had been discovered in him of wicked intent and purpose, in derogation of his civic duty, and against the honour of the council, his proper governors, and other persons of high and princely condition. Nor had he spared the Imperial Roman Emperor, our most worthy Lord, but had defamed and poisoned his name in his collected and widely-distributed chronicles, famous histories, and writings, and had brought his authority into hatred among many. By the which he had forsworn himself atrociously, and in addition had abused his position as a merchant by deception and thieving, the particulars of which were disclosed in his statement and confession '.

It might well be of interest to know a little more concerning this same Sebald Herold, who seems to have been a kind of Nuremberg Aretino on a smaller scale.

Letters of defiance or threat were also issued by the cobbler's assistant Hans Ziegler of Eschenau, whose wife, according to his statement, was ' a regular dragon, she having wounded him in the head ' and driven him to all kinds of villanies. He was sentenced to die by the sword as a rioter, and was beheaded kneeling, at his own request, on 2 September 1615 (H.).

We hear a good deal, at times, of unrestrained outbursts against authority, offences which were always seriously dealt with, even if by themselves they did not attract capital punishment. The two thieves, Hans Dorsch and Andreas Muss (1614), delivered themselves as follows in the very presence of the court :

> 'The petty nobles of Nuremberg have weighty purses and throw their money about, while we earn it with our skins'. At the place of execution Murr 'attempted to deliver a pharisaical harangue to the people, and to excuse himself, stating that he had never stolen from anybody throughout his life'. But Magister Hagendorn puts him in his place : 'It were better for him to beat his breast like the publican and cry : God be merciful to me a sinner'.

It was also related of Hans Junge, father of the thief Stephan Junge of Neumarkt, that as a soldier he and others, during the war, 'had opened their mouths too wide in the matter of pay', for which reason he had been executed. The other soldiers, too, during the same period (1614 and 1619) who were ducked[1] on the Island of Schütt were doubtless punished for similar and possibly lesser acts of insubordination.

Of actual blackmail, to give it its place here, we hear little. It is related only of an evil female (1611), that after she had dissipated her lawful husband's goods with her lover and had left him in the lurch, she returned to Gostenhof, 'and sent letters to the married men with whom she had had to do', threatening them that 'if they did not send her money she would disclose the acts of lewdness which they had committed with her'.

---

[1] [This seems to have been a punishment specially reserved for soldiers, as with us it was for scolds. A similar ducking-stool appears to have been used.]

The changed conditions of life and of domestic and social intercourse during the centuries, and the improved means of transport, particularly since the age of machinery, coupled with the great increase in population, have tended to a rigid grouping in the world of crime. As with many other present-day manifestations however, so here the isolated beginnings may be traced in the records of the past.

CHAPTER IV

OF LEWDNESS

THE subject-matter of this chapter may be said to commence with the cases of Ziegler and the woman Elizabeth Mechtlin (1611) last mentioned; that is in so far as these sexual offences have any bearing on the social life of the past. Here, again, it is not the offences as such which concern us, but rather the surrounding circumstances as they are detailed in the course of the proceedings, and especially the psychological aspect of the matter.

Magister Hagendorn devotes three closely-written pages to the case of Elizabeth Mechtlin. Her miserable offences are all detailed (compare Meister Franz, p. 70) as a result of which she was sentenced to death with the sword.

> 'For 4 days' we are told 'as we visited her from time to time, she wept for her sins and was ready and willing, she said, to go to her death, if only she could be sure that she might be a child and heir to everlasting joy and the glory of God. Indeed, what is more, she allowed it to be known at times that she was glad to leave this vile and wicked world, and would go to her death not otherwise than as to a dance. But the page was turned. The nearer she approached to death, the more sorrowful and faint-hearted did she become'.

The passage to the place of execution was accompanied by cries and prayers, with shrieks and yells, and every possible device to prolong her life. She was

82

terribly moved and difficult, so much so that her agitation caused Master Franz, a very experienced man, to bungle the execution. [Here follow the gruesome details, which can be read in the German edition, p. 41.]

Even in those rough and cruel times the death penalty was only imposed in cases where the debaucheries were of a particularly wanton nature, or where, as in the affair last mentioned, or as in the case of Barbara Schlümpfin already referred to, there was evidence of repeated adultery or incest. In cases such as these there was often a great show of piety towards the end and on the way to the scaffold. In the case of Magdalena Vischerin (1610), for instance, an incestuous adulteress, Magister Hagendorn reports :

> ' As I asked her whether she had spent the preceding night in rest and sleep, she replied that she desired to save her slumbers until she could fall asleep with the Lord Christ, and had entered her little chamber of rest and repose. On the way out she prayed continually . . . blessing the people repeatedly and fervently taking comfort, for this dear and lovely day when she was going to church. . . . When she desired to pray further at the place of execution, I told her that it was enough, upon which she prepared herself, holding her head upright for the executioner . . .'

At times, however, there was another side to the picture, as, for instance, in the case of the incestuous couple Philipp Löhner and Kunigunde Küfnerin. According to law and justice they should have been burnt alive, but on 5 March 1611, ' by favour they were first beheaded and then thrown into the fire '. Here the task of our pastor was a very difficult one, 'for the old couple knew no more than the six main principles, and even in these they were not perfect, but muddled. They did not know the number of the Godhead, nor who had saved them '. The man was soon willing to learn and to be penitent, but his companion ' sought for a long time to cover her sins and hide them with fig-leaves ', although at last there was some change. ' On the way out I comforted him, while Master Lüder comforted her. But one tried to out-run the other. He was in front at the Frauentor, but here she frequently outpaced him . . . ' (H.). Exhibitions such as this must have contributed to a very grotesque kind of entertainment.

Minor offences of this kind were generally punished by flogging. This punishment was frequently and repeatedly administered to the women of the streets whenever they broke the regulations or offended against public decency. These creatures were called after a notorious brothel ' The Neuenwald ', or possibly from a whole street, ' Newald's whores '. At times other lewd persons and frequenters of stews, among which must be reckoned the Oxen Bath[1], were flogged out of the town for ill-treating the wretched inmates.

[1] This 'bath' was in fact a brothel, as the baths frequently were. In the Ratsprotokollen [council-registers], among the archives of the town of Ingoldstadt, I discovered an original name for such places. On Wednesday after St. James (26 July) 1531 : 'for sufficient cause the following persons were forbidden the town and district, namely the Schwarzin, Beckin (and ?) the Forrester's daughter who had two husbands, but did not cohabit with them, and busied themselves with dishonest matters and knavery, and kept *Krottennester* (Kröttennester=toad-holes) which produced garbage and injurious matter '. See Grimm's Wörterbuch, V, 2422, after Krünitz, 54, 115.

LEWDNESS

I add a few examples from these walks in life for the sake of the original nicknames contained in the records.

On 18 February 1581 ' Helena Leuboldin, otherwise der Rosskäfer [the horse-beetle], who had been flogged twice, had had a finger cut off, and had been 20 times in the Loch, was for the third time flogged out of the town '.

On 12 January 1583 ' Barbara Grimmingin, a tailoress and married woman, and a burgess, who had committed lewdness with two brothers called the Schorri Morri, was flogged out of the town with rods '.

On 20 September 1586 ' Georg Schenk of Feuchtwangen, a tailor, who had committed lewdness at the Neuenwald with a prostitute called the Tücherswabel, and had taken her to wife and married her although he had already a wife and child, was flogged out of the town with rods '.

On 30 April 1596 ' Katharina Neithartin, otherwise the girl-grinder, a Neuwald's whore, was for the third time flogged out of the town with rods '.

On 22 December 1616 ' Michael Ungestüm was for the second time this year flogged out of the town with rods, and Babala, his companion, otherwise the Cornflower, and Maria Schläzin, were likewise flogged for the second time this year '.

In the council records, at the commencement of 1671, a wanton creature named Barbara Springindierosen is mentioned frequently as having been punished for her excesses.

We hear in 1531 of a kind of general punishment of men who were concerned in such matters, for in that year ' 24 burghers who had committed lewdness and adultery with the wife of Wolf König, the tanner, were confined to the Tower for four weeks on a diet of bread and water ', while Wolf König's wife was punished with the stone ' which she had to carry round the town '. Afterwards she was banished in perpetuity. In view of the period, she seems to have come off fairly lightly.

But enough of a subject which is not particularly edifying.

Meanwhile I will mention, quite shortly, the offence of polygamy, in connection with which a wire-drawer named Matthäus Sengel, ' who had four wives ', seems to have established a record. He was merely flogged out of the town with rods on 29 April 1588. Next comes sodomy which appears frequently, and which has already been referred to, then abortion— on 24 January 1719 ' an abandoned woman house-thief, and a lewd, wicked and practised abortionist' was executed with the sword—and finally we have the cases of serious offences against children which, however, do not seen to have been as common then as now. Arising out of a very serious offence of this class, it strikes us as almost humorous that the worthy Magister Hagendorn, writing of the last days of the ' German schoolmaster ' Andreas Feuerstein, who for months had abused numbers of little school-girls, can bring himself to add the following. ' He did not need any special instruction (that is in Christian doctrines) since he knew both the catechism and the exposition perfectly, as well as certain penetential psalms and the prayer of Master Eber : " Lord Jesus Christ, true Man and God ",[1] and with this he supported himself up to the end '. He was executed with the sword on 22 June 1612.[2]

Many of the depravities reflected in these extracts will be met with again in the later chapters.

---

[1] Paul Eber (1511-1569) of Kitzingen, friend and pupil of Melanchthon, Professor at the University of Wittenberg. Compare Allgemeine deutsche Biographie, V, p. 531.

[2] This is according to the official Achtbuch (MS. 217, fo. of the Amts-und Stand-bücher [Registers of office and rank] in the State Archives, Nuremberg), fo. 68b. Master Franz and M. Hagendorn, both, however, give as the date ' 23 June, Tuesday, on the eve of St. John the Baptist ' (H.).

CHAPTER V

FRAUD, DECEPTION, SWINDLING AND ADULTERATION OF FOOD

FRAUD and deception of all kinds have always played a great part in criminology, and certain special aspects of these arts will now be considered. The dominating instinct, as we shall see, in the majority of these cases which deal with sorcery, hidden treasure, exorcism, and so on, was a deliberate intent to deceive.

A few general examples must also be briefly considered in order to some extent, to support what follows. We pass from minor frauds to great ones, to the real swindlers, and close with a few examples of food adulteration.

In 1609 a sixty-year-old Vettel of Mögeldorf, who had ' a good deal deceived the people at times in money matters ', was ' as a favour pinched on both cheeks ' (M.). Equally insignificant was the swindling of the coppersmith Hans Kelsch by two women, Magdalena Greimin and the Leopoldin, whose pockets they emptied 'on the so-called Students' Square outside the Spittler Gate '. In Kelsch we have a relation of the eminent craftsman, Wolf Melchior Kelsch, a

specimen of whose work, a marvellously executed coppersmith's shield of 1723, is now in the Germanic Museum. We hear of the affair in a couple of council records in March 1712. The two women, it seems, were not ready to admit their guilt, and it was necessary ' to threaten them seriously with sharp correction on the part of the women gaolers in order to persuade them to speak the truth, or else to punish them with a few days in the Weibereisen,[1] so that they might think better of the matter. . . .'

A more scandalous fraud, affecting also a wider circle, is reported from the year 1576. It concerns four overseers, assistants of the official who collected a duty called the ' Ungeld ', a tax on wine, beer, and mead, which dates from the thirteenth century. It was their duty in the first instance to measure the casks and to act as gaugers, and they had been bribed by numerous hosts to falsify the returns to the advantage of the latter, but to the grievous damage of the town chest. When the matter was discovered the culprits were summoned one morning early to the tax office, as if there were some information to be imparted to them, and they were then and there arrested by eight town officials and taken to the Loch, where they lay for more than seven weeks. During this time their guilt had been established in the course of the proceedings, and they had in fact admitted it.

[1] [A prison for women opposite the Schütt island. It has disappeared, but the corresponding one for men, on the island itself, is still standing.]

'The rumour was generally circulated that they could only with difficulty escape with their lives. Thereupon much intercession was made on their behalf, for there were more than 36 innkeepers against whom the overseers had informed. On Tuesday, 30 March, judgment was pronounced against the overseers,[1] that by favour they and their wives and children were to be forbidden for the period of their lives to come within ten miles of the town ; the overseers were then to be flogged with rods as far as the bridge known as the Fleishbrücke, and there on a block each was to have the two first fingers of the right hand hacked off, after which they were to be whipped right out of the town . . . and this was done to the said overseers on the day named. When the overseers had suffered their punishment, the council sent again for the hosts and punished each one of them, since they had benefited greatly, with fines from 100, 150, 2, 3, 4, 5, 6, 700 to 1000 florins, which fines were imposed only by the great favour of the council, since they had deserved a severer punishment. Certain of the hosts pleaded for lenience, but they could achieve nothing. On 22 March two carriers who had assisted the hosts and the overseers in their frauds, and had kept silence, were flogged out of the town with rods '.

A much less serious offence against the revenue laws of the town is reported from the year 1655. 'Two married people from Neuhof had smuggled wine into the town '. They were banished, but were first exposed in the pillory, the man with a little cask under each arm. As against this we have in 1662 another serious fraud on the taxes. The proceedings concerned the carrier from Wöhrd, near Nuremberg, and two innkeepers of Wöhrd, the hosts of the Moor's Head and the Little Cask. I append the report of the proceedings in Frommoder's words.

[1] The MS. (M. II, pt. p. 20) has ' Wirt ' in error for ' Visierer. '.

' On 13 December (1662) the carrier of Wehrd was flogged out of the town of Nuremberg with rods, while the host of the Moor's Head, who is still (1692) living, and the hostess of the Little Cask, were placed in the pillory for a whole hour, after which they were all three banished and forbidden from now onwards for ever to approach within ten miles in length and breadth of the town and district of Nuremberg. The cause was that the carrier had brought foreign beer to certain hosts at Wehrd without declaring it, whereby they had defrauded the authorities there and especially the excise office here of large sums of money. As for the hosts of the Moor's Head and the Little Cask, they had each sold 2000 buckets without paying tax, and had stolen the duty from the authorities. The host of the Moor's Head was able, after several years, by payment of a large sum of money, to re-enter Wehrd and to be received there, but for a long period he could not go a step out of his house, and in addition he was forced to wear a rope round his neck '.

Among instances of cunning swindling, I may mention the ' remarkable prophet Hans Vatter of Mellingen ' and his marvellous doings, to whom some years ago I devoted a special study.[1] He practised his deceptions, tying himself up, trickeries with ghostly apparitions, and penitential sermons, throughout the whole of Germany, until he was exposed at Nuremberg and whipped out of the town with rods (1562).

Another swindler in the grand manner was Leibold Eckel of St. Pölten, in Austria. He fought in 1571 in the battle of Lepanto, and served also for several years as slave in the galleys. He then turned his attention to swindling. As

[1] See above, p. 23, note 6.

' Christoph von Dannhausen, Lord of Stambs, Imperial steward, knight of the Order of St. John, for so he called himself, he was on three occasions during a visit to Salzburg invited to the table of the archbishop. He came to Nuremberg during Shrovetide 1576, and was received in the house of the patrician Antoni Tetzel. He repaid this hospitality with base ingratitude by seducing Tetzel's daughter, and then disappearing from the town. But he was taken at Lichtenhof and imprisoned in the Loch. In addition to other thefts and changes of name, he used false seals, with which he deceived and befooled many eminent and respected persons, and, among them certain ladies of rank. When he heard his sentence he exclaimed; " O dear God, how fearful is mankind of public justice ! How much more should we dread to appear before God's face if we are not assured of Christ's intercession ". Upon this he was executed with the sword. He died like a Christian ' (M.).

Hans Wolf, otherwise Glaser, the son of the Nuremberg illuminator Hans Wolf, who is mentioned in Chapter I among cosmopolitan thieves, should perhaps rather be included here among rogues and adventurers, for during his career of deception, which lasted for twenty-four years, his offences were concerned mainly with serious gold frauds. To this circle belongs also ' Joseph of Lohen, or Bonnliebmann ', a grotesque figure. He was a Jew and his trick or means of livelihood was to travel up and down the country at the cost of the community, being repeatedly converted to Christianity and baptised (1682).[1] Another case is that of ' the sturdy rogue, avowed thief, and pretended alchemist ' Christian Wilhelm Cornemann. When, on 4 May 1686, he ended his

[1] Compare Bayer. Heimatschutz XXI (1925), p. 59.

life with a rope about his neck, there appeared shortly afterwards on the gallows, as Frommoder tells us, a tin plate with writing in large printed letters upon it. It was intended to be the epitaph of the criminal and read as follows :

> Observe ye wanderers a grave with three pillars,
> Which justice has set up in memory of my deeds.
> I broke the marriage vows, deceived and stole ;
> Why then should a threefold pillared grave be denied me ?
> Note from my deeds how such a life succeeds :
> For words do not always follow deeds.
> In thought I would fain have been as fleet as Mercury ;
> But the case is altered, and I am fixed immutably.

As far as the offences connected with food adulteration are concerned, they were, it seems, much less common then than now.   We hear, at times, of watered wine or beer, as for instance on 1 October 1618, when ' 14 barrels of beer had to be emptied into the waters of the Pegnitz (F.) ; also of the adulteration of spices, which formed one of the most important articles of commerce in Nuremberg, particularly in connection with saffron, which was greatly in use.   In 1444 ' Jobst Findenkern, a burgher of this town, charged with selling false saffron as genuine, was burnt alive with his saffron, and his wife was driven from the town ' (M.), and in 1619 the wealthy merchant Georg Bair who sold bad saffron, mace, and other spices, was in great peril, and only escaped death at the intercession of four counts of the Empire, and many friends, but all his condemned wares were publicly burnt.

It is probable, however, that in those days with very limited control and faulty examination, a few only of the frauds were discovered ; and of course there was much tampering with goods other than foodstuffs and luxuries. A fraud with mandrakes has already been mentioned in an earlier chapter.

Chapter VI

OF CARD-SHARPERS, COINERS AND FORGERS OF DOCUMENTS

Although we can say of certain of the offences which we have mentioned that, in proportion to the population, they were less in evidence in former times than now, yet as far as the misdeeds enumerated in this chapter are concerned, closely allied as they are with those dealt with in the preceeding chapter, it must be admitted that the exact opposite is the case.

Dice and card playing, for instance, with the accompanying tricks and deceptions, were extraordinarily common in the last centuries of the Middle Ages, and even down to comparatively modern times, and the prohibition and punishments connected with games of luck and hazard were legion.

I propose to give here, by way of supplement to the doings of Reuter Hänslein mentioned in the first chapter, a few further examples of the activities and exertions of sharpers, particularly of card-sharpers, and of the punishments meted out to them.

First of all should be mentioned a record from the year 1336 dealing with a tavern-loafer and adventurer, known generally by the nick-name Zuzu.   In this year Zuzu was forbidden ' to visit taverns, or to indulge in any kind of play for a year from Christmas.   For each breach he was to be confined in the Tower for eight days, and was then to abstain from playing and taverns for a further year ' (MS. 203, 4to, of the Amts-und Standbücher [Registers of office and rank] of the State Archives, Nuremberg, principally the reports of bans and oaths of peace from 1285 to 1337, folio 23b.)

A hundred years later we read in the records (MS. 206, fo. 32a-b) of a similar case.

" Enntlein of Tachau in Bohemia went with them (that is with certain youths suspected of robbing a boy), and all were committed to prison here and forced to confess their faults.

97

But it was not possible to get them to admit other offences beyond those already mentioned, although it was well-known that they made dice at the gallows-place, and that they were addicted to playing, swindling, and begging. Therefore, on account of what had occurred, all four had to swear an oath of peace against the townspeople and their goods and were then allowed to go free. Actum feria IIII, p. Martini (17 November) 1434 fo. 1c, lx '. (The contemporary Red Book which, from the formal nature of the hand-writing appears to date from the beginning of the fifteenth century.)

Zuzu and Ännelein of Dachau may, to some extent, be regarded as the spiritual ancestors of that boundless company of suspected or convicted sharpers with which the records of the succeeding centuries are crowded. The master-mind may well have been the Reuter-Hänslein, already mentioned, who played a part from time to time in proceedings other than his own. Another rogue was ' Friederich Werner, otherwise the Heffner-Fridla ', a robber and murderer, who was executed with the sword by Master Franz Schmidt (see his Diary) on 11 February 1585. During the enquiry he implicated thirty-five ' criminals and housebreakers ' as his accomplices and receivers (compare Appendix III), adding, ' these companions are all rogues who cut purses and play with three or five dice and with the salt (?), and once the Reuter-Hänslein won from this speaker all his clothes '.

From this passage it appears that the expressions and games which are referred to in the proceedings are often difficult to identify to-day. The same remark holds good for a passage from Murr's manuscript from

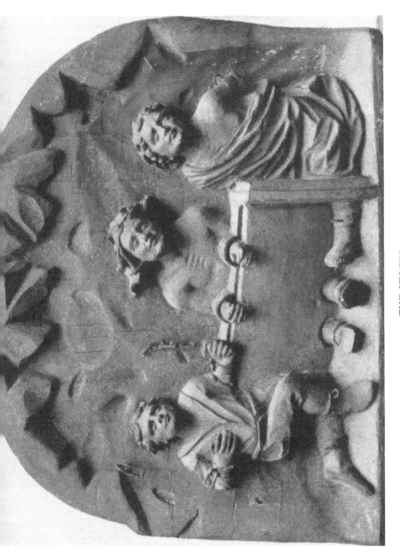

THE STOCKS
From a coloured carving. Germanic Museum, Nuremberg, about 1700

[to face p. 98

the year 1594 concerning a sharper named Hans
Gesert of Kitzingen, who ' by means of a board—
possibly a chess-board—and three or four stones
(chess-men) won four thalers from the people. He
let fall also a gilded counter among passers-by,
claiming half its value when it was found. For this
he was flogged out of the town with rods '.

In the following year another sharper, ' Georg
Rosenzweig, otherwise the Rosala ', was whipped, and
two years later, on 24 October 1597, having repeated
the offence and committed also lewdness and perjury,
he lost his fingers. ' And as no stocks were available
they were set up specially on the stone bridge (the
present Maxbrücke), but the people called them the
calvinists' pulpit, and they were removed ' (M.).

The punishment for coining was a dreadful one both
before and after the introduction of the Carolina—
death by fire. But in the sixteenth century, as far as
I have ascertained, it was invariably changed by favour
to death by the sword or strangulation, followed
immediately or later by the burning of the corpse.
In one solitary case (1617), there does seem to have been
an actual burning alive, but this arose from the clumsi-
ness of the Löwe or hangman's assistant, who did
not twist the strangling-stick fast enough, so that the
victim, who was bound to the stake, actually suffered
the tortures of death by fire. The criminal was the
coiner Georg Karl Lamprecht of Mainbernheim, and
I have described this dreadful execution in the study

referred to in the preface to this book. It was Master Franz's last and most horrible official execution.

As against this, on 4 September 1572, Leonhard Kollner, ' a goldsmith and burgher of this town ', was by favour beheaded and then burnt, together with his two accomplices, the coiners Michael Hoffmann, the father, host of the Blue Horse, and Michael Hoffmann, the son, a dealer in fats, for whom the father had cut the dyes necessary for the coining operations. On 11 July 1598 the coiner Hans Kolb of Altdorf, a tile-maker, ' called otherwise the long tiler or brother Weichnit ', who had, in addition, a number of crimes of the most serious character on his conscience, was first broken with the wheel and then burnt. He had attempted to kill himself by biting his arm, in order, as he hoped, to bleed to death, and on his way out he refused all spiritual comfort ; ' he knew it all, he said, and did not want to hear it. They were making his head mad '. ' How he died God knows ' (M.).

The Malefactors' Books also report a case in which a coiner was interceded for and freed. ' On 19 December in the year 1677 Hans Nicolaus Göbel, a burgher and goldsmith of this town, who struck 50 whole, 6 half, and 16 quarter guldens from the Öttingen dye, and was condemned to death, was subsequently freed ' (M.).

A clever goldsmith, particularly when in financial difficulties, had special temptation to coin false money.

The name of a great craftsman must now be mentioned in connection with the crime of forgery, and a few words may be added from the original documents concerning him. But Veit Stoss, the 'cunning sculptor', as he is called in the Malefactors' Books, had on his side some of the elements of natural justice when he forged the bond of his faithless friend Jakob Paner, copying his handwriting exactly and reproducing his seal by 'subtle arts'. According to the letter of the law, however, the punishment for a serious offence of this nature was infallibly death, and it was due solely to his art that the penalty was changed to public branding 'through both cheeks' (1503). To what extent this shameful punishment ate into the heart of the aging master, and how he devoted the last thirty years of his long life without ceasing, and with all the forces he could command, towards securing his rehabilitation is now a matter of history.

We have no other case in our Malefactors' Books to equal the forgery of Veit Stoss. But the punishment even in serious cases grew milder with the years. Thus on 10 November 1596 the 'burgher and goldsmith Andreas Petri, called otherwise the Swiss'—we are concerned once again with a goldsmith—who had forged seals and title-deeds, but without defrauding anyone', and who had conducted himself otherwise in a criminal and unlawful manner (compare Master Franz's account), was merely flogged out of the town with rods.

The individuals who pass through our records with forged 'letters of fire', that is with fraudulent proofs that they had lost their possessions through fire, or with other documents, often only too clumsily forged, would amount to a great company. Indeed, in times of domestic hardship, and particularly in times of war, such cases tend to multiply to an alarming extent. It is only possible here to mention two masters of the art, a cobbler's apprentice of Brunswick, who in January 1680, on the strength of forged birth certificates importuned all kinds of people to assume the obligations of sponsors, although, as it turned out, he had never been married, and a cleric, ' who had laboured much with forged letters and seals, whereby many people were defrauded of their money '. For these offences the cleric was exposed in the pillory (April 1640) ' and a Latin N (=Nuremberg) was burnt into his cheeks ', after which he was banished from the town.

But it is not necessary to consider this group of petty swindlers any further.

Chapter VII

OF MAGIC, TREASURE-SEEKERS, WITCHES,
EXORCISTS AND BLASPHEMERS

SINCE the life of the past centuries and all its movements and conceptions were influenced and surrounded by superstition we should expect it to find a place in our official records, nor is it strange that the cult and forbidden practice of unnatural arts, with magic of all kinds, should be regarded as evidence of a pact with the devil. For although there were always exceptional persons whose conception of God's power in the world was lofty and unfettered, yet the great mass of the people, and even the upper classes, were sunk for the most part in heathen stupor. There is evidence, indeed, of such conditions to-day, although legal conceptions and interpretations are tending more and more to throw off such restraints.

At one time, that is in the period of which we are speaking, even the judges were often the victims of delusion and superstition. It happens therefore that not infrequently our records treat of the most extra-ordinary and even laughable affairs with the greatest solemnity, as if they contained the whole essence of the matters which were being deliberated. To the credit, however, of common sense in general it must be admitted that, as far as the old Nuremberg legal system is concerned, this odd manifestation does not seem to have greatly increased the methods of punishment. In most cases involving the offences set out at the head of this chapter, there were generally other serious crimes which must have greatly influenced the course of justice. Only notorious and open blasphemy was dealt with by itself, although, even here, we are tempted at times, as with much else relating to the legal systems of the past, to attribute the offence to imperfect understanding and spiritual darkness.

It is therefore not unnatural in considering these offences to look for evidence of magic and superstition. How much rubbish of this kind was—and is still—associated with the trade of thieving ! The hand of a newly-born child would secure the burglar against the risk of anyone waking in the house and taking him in the act, and we know a good deal of the appalling methods adopted by thieves, who stopped at nothing to possess themselves of these gruesome charms which had, by the way, to be ignited before use. A monster of this kind was the thief and vagabond Sebastian Grebel of Grupenhofen (1601), who, to attain his ends, murdered a number of pregnant women. Nor was this by any means the grossest of these delusions. Others professed ' to know of a root, and if one took it in the mouth and merely blew at a lock, it sprang open ' (A., for the year 1612). Others again attempted to make themselves immune from bullets by carrying on their persons a fragment of a skull or ' a piece of rope from the gallows on which a thief had been hanged '. The rope of a church bell, if worn by a thief or robber, was believed to ensure that nothing would be disclosed under torture.

The same delusions affected also murderers, sexual offenders, and swindlers of all kinds. But instead of giving further instances I will reproduce here in extenso a typical case, in which crime was mixed with superstition, and let it speak for itself. I have selected the record of the confirmed church robber Sixt Kuhn of Stein, a server at Mass at Gründlach, who was executed with the sword on 18 July 1622. The burning of the church at Gründlach had given an opportunity for his arrest, and the patron of the church, ' his master, the noble and upright Carol Pfinzing ', appeared in person against him as accuser. It seems from the enquiry

' that he, Kuhn ', as he is called in the Achtbuch (MS. 219 fo. Nuremberg State Archives, fo. 195), ' a disreputable magician, church-robber and thief, had frequently admitted that he had scandalously abused the consecrated Host, hanging the elements round the necks of brute beasts, and between their horns, using also bell-clappers to make a pretended medicine for the vomit. He had also taken wood from the coffin-stand of a woman who had died in her first child-bed, and had dug it up and scraped the wood among the horses' food. He had further drunk from the skulls of dead people, which skulls he had also dug up, and had appropriated baptismal water with intent to throw it to swine, and had further called up the evil one by night to discourse with him upon hidden matters. In addition he had at all times abused the holy and blessed Trinity in an outrageous manner, all of which according to Holy Writ was blasphemy and a mortal sin against the Holy Ghost, deserving the highest punishment both according to spiritual and worldly justice '.

He had, moreover, abused his post as server by committing the most odious and forcible church-robbery. After execution with the sword his body was to be thrown upon a pyre and burnt to ashes.

So much for the judgment. I add this following from the enquiry.

AN EXECUTION, 1489
Bürgher-Bibliothek, Lucerne

[to face p. 106

WITCHES, BLASPHEMERS

'It was objected

' Shall he disclose his magical practices ? He says that the innkeeper Hans Weigel of Gründlach knew an art, if a man was deprived of his virility, to restore it again, and the details were as follows. Take white chicory, which must be dug between 11 and 12 on St. James's day, roots of violets, the filings of a bell-clapper, something white grated which tasted like a root, but the innkeeper did not want to tell him what this was. The infusion was then to be drunk until the patient was restored, but he was to be told as well that he must also pray fervently. This practice, says the speaker, was observed by him, and the innkeeper gave him the half of what he earned by it and they enjoyed it together. But the speaker could not make the concoction, for the innkeeper was present and mixed the roots with the bell-filings, which he and the innkeeper always fetched together, going together to the tower. It was the innkeeper also who filed the bell-clappers. . . .'

' . . . And he, the speaker, knew also a remedy for the headache and falling-sickness (?) which was as follows. " Stand on wood, look upon wood, look out upon a green twig. Expiate this fever ; expiate this sickness (?), expiate this headache, which shall be counted to you for penance. It shall be to you for 72 times (?). In the name of the Father, Son and Holy Ghost, Amen." And anyone with headache must say three Paternosters, three Ave Marias, and three Creeds. This charm he had from his mother.'

These extracts will be sufficient, I think, to show the overwhelming power of superstitious beliefs, or black magic, in many minds at that time. Nor is Magister Hagendorn able to free himself entirely from such influences, as appears from the passage in the proceedings against the silver-thief Hans Schenker of Trossenberg (1609). Speaking of his Christian admonitions, he says : ' I showed him also the devil in the blue glass ', implying, it would seem, that Satan could be laid by the heels, exorcised, and deprived of his powers. (Compare Bayer. Heimschutz, XXI (1925), p. 55.)

As might be expected these delusions were more general among the executioners' assistants than among the common people. After the execution of the adulterer and poisoner Hans Otzmann (1674), the assistant collected the blood in an earthern pot, and gave it to drink to people suffering from epilepsy, ' whereby they became cured, whole, and sound ' (F.). ' Three peasants, a youth, and a girl drank the blood which was still warm ' (M.). It is related of the thief Georg Perger from Tyrol, who was hanged on 9 October 1677, that ' during the first night the executioner and his assistants took him down, cut pieces from him as they pleased, and hanged him up again, which thing was seen by the laundresses near by who saw them going about the gallows with lanterns ' (M.). And other curious examples of the popular craving for quack medicine—for this is undoubtedly what it was—could be gathered in vast numbers from our records.

But I will return to magic, or ' magic in chief ' as it might be called, and instead of examining the matter in detail, I will give here a few examples only, adding further parallels from folklore and outside sources as occasion arises. The literature dealing with the various phases of pretended arts and sciences and occult manifestations is so vast and widely disposed that not long ago a bibliographer maintained that its capacity exceeded the sum total of all the publications in the remaining branches of literature.

In the case of Peter Hoffmann, who by favour was executed with the sword on 6 March, 1604, his thefts—his speciality was to take honey and bees which he did with the help of his associate Brigitta—and his magical arts are about evenly distributed.   Of the latter, in the course of the enquiry, we hear as follows :

' *It was objected*

' It appeared from the skull and bones found with him that he was a cursed sorcerer who busied himself with incantations and conjurations, and, as it was proved, had with the aid of his wicked sorceries transported his companion from Gemundt as far as Schwarzenlohe.   He would do well to disclose what he knew of such arts.

He affirmed that he had in truth no dealings with forbidden things, and none had ever heard or perceived such things of him.   The skull, which he had taken innocently at Erlang from the prison, he used to give drinks to the sick against falling, and when they took it penitently they were recovered. This was, he hoped, not magic.   When his Brigitta, who had been with him at Schwarzenlohe, ran away from him and went to Gemundt to the Landsknechten, he was anxious to have her again.   But she would not come, and he learnt from his boy that if he tied some of her clothing to a bell and let it ring, she could not stop away.   He took therefore her loin-cloth (salva venia), and with the consent of the Burgo-masters he hung it on the bell and let it ring, but whoever came it was certainly not Brigitta, and as the procseding was ineffective he sent his boy after her, and he brought her back with him '.

We learn also much concerning the devilish practices

of the impious coiner Georg Carl Lamprecht (1617, see above), and the official record supplements the report of Magister Hagendorn in a very interesting manner. (See MS. 217 fo. Nuremberg State Archives, fo. 326a.)

'It was objected

'It was impossible to credit his story, for there was much information to show that not only was he himself a true sorcerer and conjurer of devils, holding the burghers and people in subjection, besides being (fo. 326b) addicted to devilish arts, but in addition, he had attached himself to the old Eisenbeissin and had married her, and had contrived with her help every kind of adultery and whoredom. Whether all the sorceries which he is alleged to have practised were true, what persons he had seduced therewith, and what dealings he had had with the Eisenbeissin, these were matters upon which it was desired to have his report.

He says that none would be able to establish that he had ever in his life learnt or practised witchcraft or conjuration. Once a man from Bamberg, called the Taubenschneider, had given the speaker a bundle containing a white powder which he was to hang about his neck as a charm against shot. This powder was burnt before Strasburg when the camp was burnt. In addition, the Eisenbeissin had given him the Passauer art written on paper and wafers, which he was to use, but he paid no attention to them, and never made use of them. As for the Eisenbeissin, he came to know her through Plattner of Kitzingen, who persuaded him that he should first go with him to a herb-woman at Bamberg. Since she was not in her house he came with his companion to Nuremberg, for this herb-woman was sister to Köpflein's mother. When they went to find her in the Köpflein's house they met with her for the first time, and enquired whether she had not some springwort, but they were referred to the Eisenbeissin who was said to be a woman skilled in such matters. This, says the speaker, was the first occasion on which he became acquainted with the Eisenbeissin. She told them that if she had a white adder it would be better than springwort, and that she knew of a grove near Neuenmark where was a medlar-tree beneath which was a white adder. Thereupon she persuaded this speaker to go with Köpflein and his brother to Neuenmark and to dig for the white adder in a peasant's garden in a village near the town. This speaker copied from Höhn's book on a sheet of paper the charm for the conjuration of the adder. This he read three times in the name of the Trinity, so that the adder should not stir. Then the Köpflein dug to about a knee's depth, but as they found nothing they departed again. Upon this the speaker, when he returned, remained with the Eisenbeissin '. (Then follows an account of his companionship with her). . . .

' It was objected

' If he knew nothing of the arts of sorcery, how came it to be proved that he had imparted certain of these arts to the Köpflein, and had also given him, among other things, a fragment of a skull and other human bones ? He had better disclose whence he obtained them and for what good purpose.

He says that he obtained the piece of skull and other bones from the dog-killer at Kitzingen, who told him that they were good for shots if hung about the neck, and that they came from a poor sinner. He gave him a Reichsthaler for them. This speaker then tied them to a dog to test them (fo. 328a) while his brother fired at the dog. But when it appeared that the dog was dead, and that the charm had not saved it, he took little notice of the business further and gave the charm to Köpflein. And when he saw that the deeds and boasts of these vagabonds were all feigned and imagined and could teach him no arts which would bring him anything, but, on the contrary, only involved him in expenses, and he was thus defrauded of his own, he did not desire to have anything further to do with them. . . .'

Another female worthy to be placed in the same category as the Eisenbeissin referred to above, whose springwort and adder-magic we shall encounter again, was ' Sabina Köstlin, a goldspinster, called otherwise the Schlenderwina ', whom we meet with in the year 1657. She attracted notice by her godless and scandalous life and wanderings about the town, all of which she admitted, and ' which was sufficiently proved by sworn and worthy testimony '.

> ' She had indulged in superstitious practices, using unheard of curses and blasphemies ; she had threatened her husband and son-in-law with injury to life and limb, which was equivalent to sorcery, and had sinned grievously in other ways against God, the authorities, and the whole Christian community here. Therefore she has deserved exemplary punishment. It was adjudged accordingly that on Wednesday early, at the time of the morning sermon, this Köstlin should be placed before the church of the Preaching Friars, barefooted, with a rod in her hand, and then carried outside the town by the town officials, and should take an oath never to return within ten miles of the district. Later, when the official had left her, and she had crossed the Fischbach behind the gallows, this same Köstlin was met by children and foully bespattered with filth, sand and earth, thrust here and there, and then chased behind the Hummelstein far into the woods, as the same may be read in the printed song concerning her. Later she returned into the town and settled there, and practised her spinning as before ' (M.).

Apart from sorcerers and witches, whose incantations sound very ridiculous, and whose charms and formulas were often mistakenly recorded by the clerk, we have special mention also of purveyors of blessings and seers, and above all of treasure seekers, male and female. The malpractices of the Eisenbeissin already mentioned had reference to deceptions of this kind, and no definite line of demarcation can be drawn between them, and the witchcraft and other matters dealt with in this chapter.

In the matter of treasure-seeking, as we know it from the Nuremberg Malefactors' Books, the white adder plays an important part, and although it is not within the scheme of this book to consider examples drawn from outside sources, I may still be allowed to remark that neither in ancient or modern references to treasure-seeking, as far as my enquiries extend, has the white adder anything like the same significance as here.

There is in general much talk concerning dragons, snakes, or dogs who guard the hidden treasure, and of course, when the ground had been opened with the aid of springwort and other magical roots, in order to come at the treasure, these creatures had to be charmed and exorcised. We learn also that flowering ferns—called adder ferns—worn on the person, acted as a certain bait to adders, and were even sovereign against 'a very lovely maiden with human form down to the navel, but below the navel she was shaped like a monstrous snake', which creature guarded a certain treasure with the aid of two dogs.[1] The delusion as a whole may have had its origin in the much quoted passage in the Bible, Psalm 58, 4-5, dealing with the godless flatterers of Saul: 'Their poison is like the poison of a serpent: they are like the deaf adder that

---

[1] Magiologia, Christliche Warnung für dem Aberglauben und Zauberey . . . der fürwitzigen Welt zum Ekel, Scheusal und Underweisung fürgestellt durch Bartholomaeum Anhorn, Pfarrer der Evangelischen Kirchen und Gemeind zer Bischoffszell, Basle 1674, p. 861.

stoppeth her ear. Which will not hearken to the voice of charmers, charming never so wisely '. Ecclesiastes, chapter 10, verse 11, and Jeremiah, chapter 8, verse 17, were also quoted on occasion. But where the white adder comes from—possibly it is a reminiscence of the lovely maiden already mentioned—I have so far been unable to discover.

However, I will now give some further extracts from the Nuremberg records. A complete and avaricious rogue who quite obviously had no belief in her own rubbish, was Elizabeth Aurholdin, a wooden-legged seamstress of Vilseck, who was executed with the sword on 1 February 1598. Master Franz, who cut off her head, describes, albeit in a rather muddled way, her various offences, and mentions also the white adder, a specimen of which she was said to carry about with her hidden in one of her legs. Her activities are described in greater detail in Murr's manuscript. It appears from the enquiry that she once deceived three men with the story ' that hundreds of years ago a castle stood on the Glatzenstein, but that it had disappeared. In its place was a hole in which was an iron chest full of treasure, and if they could dig up a white adder for her, she would charm the treasure so that it would float on the water, and this they believed although she had invented it '. A carpenter of Feucht, who went about with a divining rod, helped her with the treasure-seeking, but it was, of course, in vain. She was much sought after and in request, and her grotesque and ridiculous pretences actually ensured her reception as a guest in the houses of persons of rank. She was received, for instance, in the castle of the nobleman Jörg Walnröder at Ziegenburg, with whom she came to an understanding that ' she should lie in with her present child in his castle '. Thus, in fact, so the record continues, ' she was brought to bed there and demanded of the before-mentioned nobleman and also of Martin Sigmund von Rabenstein that they should stand as sponsors. . . '.

' Item, she gave out that she was a golden Sunday child and carried a white adder about with her hidden in her right leg, with the aid of which she could see and discover all hidden treasure which disclosed itself to her, and when the earth opened one could see inside, and behold, it was all fire. . . .'

The credulity of the people, especially when quickened by avarice and greed, was certainly very remarkable. Thus, on 20 March 1605, Anna Dammerin of Pegnitz, ' who had deceived the people with stories of hidden treasure, and had stolen much, was flogged out of this town with rods '.

Closely allied with sorcerers, but more conscientious than the bulk of treasure-seekers in that, as a rule, they believed implicitly in their own powers, were the witches and cunning women. And it is to the lasting credit of Nuremberg that it never gave itself up to the burning of witches. How dreadfully this fury raged elsewhere at the end of the sixteenth century is shown by the proceedings against the smeller-out of witches, Friedrich Stigler of Abenberg, who was executed with the sword on 28 July 1590 in Nuremberg, on the score (as Master Franz expresses it) of his wicked crying after and charges against honest women, and for other like crimes. Considerations of space prevent me from examining this interesting case in detail, and I must content myself by referring to Master Franz's account, and to Knapp's *Das Lochgefängnis*. p. 40.

Nevertheless, the criminal law of Nuremberg had to reckon with two thorough-going witches or devil's-dams. The first was Margaretha Mautererin, who on 26 April 1659 ' was first by special favour tied to a post and strangled and then burnt to powder and ashes '. She was the wife of one of the town watchmen. Her first husband, Georg Staudinger, was the hangman's assistant, or Löwe. It appeared during the enquiry

'that eight years ago, during the lifetime of her former husband, in vain contempt of God and in neglect of his help and almighty power, and in her desire for worldly riches and miserable profit, she had summoned to her help, in his own person, Satan, the bitter enemy of God and of mankind. Then, at his appearance and by his temptation, she had with dreadful blasphemies renounced the most holy and veritable Trinity, had delivered herself up to the devil and had had carnal connection with him. Twice at the celebration of the holy sacrament she had taken the consecrated wafer from her mouth and offered it to the devil, and by his command had attempted and approved the injury to body and life of several persons through witchcraft . . .' (U.).

Frommoder, apparently an eyewitness, adds the following to his fairly detailed report. ' This Maria

Wo Raub u. Mord geschah, wie grausam er gewesen, Auch wie der Thäter floh und im Gefängniß lag,

Zeigt hier der Augenschein; u. was man nie gelesen, Legt nun die Wahrheit selbst durch diese Schrift an Tag.

Das Todes Urtheil wird allhier gerecht gesprochen: Es soll des Mörders Leib das Rad von unten auf

Zu seinem Lohn empfahug nun wird die That gerochen, Und also endet sich des Sünders Lebenslauf.

ERLANGEN,
gedruckt und zu finden bey Johann Dietrich Michael Kammerer, Universit. Buchdr.

THE HISTORY OF A CRIME

[to face p. 116

(Margaretha) Mautiererin (or Mautererin) was carried out in a chair by the watch to the common place of execution, since she was not to be trusted on foot.'

Three weeks after this execution, on 17 May 1659, another witch, Maria Regina Mettmannin, 'was first by special favour executed with the sword, after which her body, together with the head, was burnt with fire to powder and ashes'. The offences were practically the same as in the last case, but in addition to the injury to property, which she contrived with Satan's help, it is stated that 'finally, by command of the evil one, she had abducted a young and innocent girl of 10½ years and had delivered her into his hands. . . .' (U.).

It is to be noticed that in this and the former case there was actual physical injury to the witches' victims, and this doubtless influenced the judgment of the court.

Very similar in character were the conjurers and exorcists, who might be called the male counterparts of the witches. Thus, in 1551, we hear of a sheep-stealer, Georg Fischer, and the devil's charm which he is said to have learnt from his father: 'Säudreck, Säudreck'. Again, in 1613, we have an account of the numerous thefts by Georg Bruckner, 'who at Krems, being moved thereto by magical black arts, had denied the holy Trinity and had bound himself to the devil by a dreadful oath' (H.). Such were his ravings and outcries during his imprisonment in the

Tower that the very roarings of the devil were thought to be within him, and Master Holzschuher, who lived close by, could not sleep for the noise. How finally, in the Loch prison, and upon his last journey, he was transformed from a 'raging wolf' into a 'patient lamb' will appear in my projected edition of Magister Hagendorn's Memorial. The history also of the trooper Melzer 'who concealed three Hosts about him, devoured three children's hearts, and carried three children's hands on his person' (M.), can be passed over here, since this 'evil fellow' was not executed at Nuremberg, but at Amberg on 29 April 1719. The case of Christian Schumann, 'who was born at Belgern in Meissen', may however be mentioned in greater detail, for Schumann was a Nuremberg mercenary and was taken in 1687 after he had broken into a beer cellar with an accomplice. The two were forced

> 'to run the gauntlet, but it had no effect upon him. With the help of Satan he contrived to escape from the prison, but he was captured on the following day by the town gate and taken to the Loch. Here a tablet was found on him from which it appeared that he had renounced the fear of God and his holy baptismal vows, had often called up the devil, to whom he bound himself with his blood, for which causes he was executed by favour with the sword (on 20 March 1688) ' (M.).

To such devil's associates belong also the blasphemers, of whom we hear much in the Nuremberg Malefactors' Books.

As early as 1337, ' on Wednesday before St. James's Day' (23 July) ' Jördel the bag-maker' was banished for ever and forbidden ' on his neck ', i.e. under pain of death, to approach within five miles of the outskirts, for ' abusing God ', and ' because he had sworn an oath of peace' (MS, 203, 4to of the Amts-und Stand-bücher [Registers of office and rank], State Archives, Nuremberg, fo. 25a). At a later date blasphemers, as a rule, had their tongues torn out, and the tongues were then nailed to the ear-pillory on the bridge known as the Fleischbrücke as a warning (1529, 1542, 1550, 1558, etc.). From the last case, however, in 1558, it is to be noticed that by then only the tip of the tongue was cut off for it is related of Albrecht Strasser, the son of a burgher and carpenter, ' who blasphemed God most terribly, and cursed in a horrible manner while playing on the Hallerwiese ', and who was therefore sentenced to this punishment, ' that he spoke better afterwards than before, for previously he had stammered somewhat ' (M.).

The blasphemies themselves are also recorded at times. Andreas Brunner, a burgher and glazier of Altdorf, during a thunderstorm, called ' God in Heaven an old scoundrel who had lost his money at play and cards, and now wanted to recover it with bullets (? ninepins) ' (M.). He also, after standing in the pillory for a quarter of an hour, was deprived of ' a piece of his tongue ' on the Fleischbrücke (19 April 1593). As against this Barbara Catharina Cranzin, a weaver, who as a Calvinist had married a Lutheran in Nuremberg, and who asked her husband, when he went to God's table, 'whether he had been to the pigsty' was 'exposed before St. Sebald's church' (M., on 28 November 1566).

With these examples we can now leave the subject.

Chapter VIII

THE WORLD AT LARGE

Under this heading, after having examined the most diverse records of crime, I propose to survey briefly, from the point of view of social history, certain individuals, circumstances and happenings and their part, now great, now small, in the administration of justice. I shall continue to make use of the authorities mentioned in my introduction, and must of necessity indicate rather than describe, since a closer examination of the material, as well as any attempt to grapple with outside sources, would take me too far from the subject of this work.

It would be of considerable psychological interest to know something of the outlook and mentality of the councillors who acted as prison magistrates, and of the other officials who took part in the proceedings. Unfortunately our records tell us nothing about them, nor about the judges who seem to rise above the rest with a kind of cold detachment and without personality. We have their names inscribed in formal script at the opening of each enquiry, and nothing more. During the course of the proceedings, as we have already seen, crowds of individuals make their appearance, either as injured parties, witnesses, accessories, and receivers, and so forth, all of whom have some relation to the matters in hand. Jews at Ottensoos, Kersbach, Schnaittach, and many other places, and above all at Fürth, appear frequently as purchasers of stolen goods, until at times this business of receiving, which was openly countenanced, gives one the impression of an organized and licensed trade.

The frauds and deceptions we meet with are numerous and varied. In 1614, during the proceedings against the child-murderess Anna Emels (see above), mention is made of 'a female Swabian weaver dwelling in the Schwabenburg, opposite the Fröschturm', who maintained herself by making ruffles—it was the time of the frilled and pleated hooped collars—and offered shelter to the girls who assisted her. These girls had then to serve the customers 'who came for her collars'.

Nor were the prisoners entirely removed from the happenings and excitements of the outside world. They might receive visits in the Loch from their relations and friends, and entertain them, and, as appears from Hagendorn's report of the case of Barbara Schlümpfin (compare Appendix I) they were not unduly constrained in their habits and lives. When Georg Bair, the wealthy merchant and seller of false saffron, was imprisoned, the clerics were expressly instructed and warned by two members of the council that they were not to receive presents from the prisoner, nor carry presents to him. Only his father confessor, Master Demminger, was suffered to take delight in a gift of flowers, which was sent to him with gracious words. When judgment was postponed, the clergy were invited by the prisoner to partake of wine with him. There were cookings and bakings in the gaoler's apartments until a most savoury smell arose, and Bair gave a banquet at which 'some 20 measures of wine' were consumed (H.).

There was an attempt at concession even in matters of toilet, and the authorities, as we have seen in the case of the thief Georg Merz and his 'black cap', allowed the delinquents considerable latitude in their wishes. Thus the adulteress, Barbara Zeilerin (1605) was suffered to wear her straw hat, not only in prison, but also on the way to execution, while the poacher Veit Flath, wore on his last journey (1607) ' a wreath which his sister, in service at Wöhrd, had sent to him as a blessing ' (H.). A gipsy woman (1733) was allowed, before her own execution, to lay a bunch of flowers on her lover's wheel, that is on the wheel with which he had been broken (Knapp, *Lochgefängnis*, p. 77).

In addition to the goaler and his family, the persons most generally about the criminals under sentence of death, at least during their last days, were the clerics charged with the care of their souls. These worthy men had until well after the second half of the sixteenth century, for the most part, their own free quarters, as one would say to-day, in the Loch. It was not until 1557 that ' the serving of meals to the chaplains was suspended and each one of them received two gulden. Hans Öler, harness-master at the Peunt, was then the Loch gaoler ' (M.).

Naturally these clerics had a difficult time with some of the criminals who were often little better than brute beasts. We have met with several examples of violence and obstinacy—I recall the case of Georg Merz—and the intended publication of Hagendorn's Memorial will provide further instances which are important from the point of view both of psychology and medicine. It is sufficient to indicate here the description by Frommoder of the wild behaviour and bearing of Hans Schrenker, further details of which are given in Hagendorn's report (see Bayr. Heimatschütz, XXI (1925), pp. 55f).

> 'This same Hans Schrenker', says Frommoder, 'was a very godless person who absolutely and entirely refused to pray. At his going out he ran so strongly and rapidly that neither of the clerics who had spoken with him were able to keep up with him, and the executioner had to hold and pull the rope with which he was secured with all his power and might, but it was all useless, and he continued to run at top speed.'

The clerics took endless trouble with the sinners committed to their care. They enquired concerning their knowledge and familiarity with the catechism, the Bible and books of hymns, all of which they diligently expounded, seeking with great earnestness to enlarge their charges' acquaintance with these foundations of the Lutheran belief. Their one aim was to edify unbelievers and renew their faith, to strengthen the doubting and the hopeless with the word of God, and to admonish and punish the obstinate and callous, striving at all times to establish a trust in divine mercy and to prepare the way by penitence and contrition for a Christian death. To save the soul of the poor sinner from eternal damnation was the single purpose which Magister Hagendorn had in mind. Here are a few examples.

The precious-stone cutter, Valentin Golter, who was executed with the sword on 30 December 1557 for grievous offences committed against his second wife and her family—the matter is not clear, even with the help of the official record—said the Lord's Prayer on his way to the place of execution and sang 'Come ye to me, says God's own Son'. 'Finally, on the Rabenstein, he said " I am done to death by a whore ", meaning his wife. Otherwise he was diligent in hearing God's word. God knows how he died ' (M.).

On 17 September 1560 the child-murderess, Barbara Segerin, was drowned. ' In matters of faith she was like a heathen, but she died at last in good hope of salvation.' In 1572 we learn of another woman charged with child-murder, Katharina Federreuterin that ' she was a simple person and did not know how to pray ' (M.) The confirmed thief Hans Seubold, of Schlammersdorf, ' showed himself to be very hard and stubborn, and his heart was not to be softened ' (H.). Finally, however, he too gave way (1611).

In 1611 an incorrigible thief had to be admonished not to be so sanctimonious (A.) ; another thief in 1612 ' not only knew his catechism and exposition, but also many comforting texts and psalms '. He was therefore ' one who knew the Lord's will, but did not do it, and was, in consequence, doubly worthy of stripes ' (H.). The thief Hans Drechsler of Bayreuth (1614) on the other hand, knew nothing of the catechism and such matters, but with the aid of the keeper he learnt more in the last three or four days than in all the rest of his life. ' Of a certainty he was about to go straight to Christian Paradise. He turned to the waiting people when the rope was already round his neck with these words :

"God bless you and the leaves and the grass,
    And everything I leave behind,

Say a Paternoster for me. To-day I shall pray for you in Paradise ". It is to be believed that he died well and like a Christian ' (H.).

When the house-breaker Paulus Kraus (1616) climbed the ladder to the gallows, and announced that he was about to atone for his sins, the strict theologian Magister Hagendorn objected at the last moment, 'that as for his sins, the Lord Christ had already atoned and paid for them. He should commend his soul to God, his heavenly father, which he then did '.

A man who was tolerably instructed from the beginning was the thief Stephan Jung, who fell out with an accomplice in the Tetzel chapel of the Aegidien Church when they were dividing some plunder, and in a passion stabbed a companion called Alexander Baumheckelein. After the deed, he and the two other thieves gave the murdered man three kisses. The murderer then surrendered himself to justice and was eventually sentenced by favour to be beheaded with his two accomplices, Hans Münch and Hans Jakob Dionysii, whereupon all three fell on their knees and praised God and the authorities with uplifted hands. 'Hans Jakob and Jung ', says Magister Hagendorn, ' were able to give a sufficient account of their beliefs, but the third, that is Münch, knew little. He could not say the six principles, and denied that he knew how to answer to other matters of doctrine. Nevertheless, he prayed for God's grace on several occasions, and we strove to be patient with him, since he desired to learn what he did not know. This we did and brought him as far as we could in the knowledge of the Lord Christ '.

At times there are evidences of a certain rivalry and doggedness among the official clergy, the latter especially when it was a question of converting a papist to the Lutheran creed and thus saving a soul. Magister Hagendorn relates many such attempts and labours, which at times were crowned with complete success. How deep the new religious convictions went we cannot say, but when we read of a ' wicked house-thief ', Andreas Muss, a catholic, who was converted by the two clerics to evangelistic beliefs, and received the communion at the hand of Master Lüder—the execution was obviously postponed for a week so that the instruction might be completed—it is difficult to suppress a smile, for Magister Hagendorn reports as follows :

> ' He had several times intimated that his heart's wish was to live for another quarter of a year so that he might inform himself more thoroughly in his recent studies of the Evangelists the better to taste their sweetness. Upon which I replied that the good God had fulfilled his wish and that he had extended his life for several days. . . .'

The two clerics received in this case for their added instruction ' an honorarium in duplo '. Well-disposed delinquents also left the pastors a few gulden in their wills, if they were suffered by the council to make them.

It appears, as Knapp says (*Das Lochgefängnis*, p. 53), 'that the last days of the poor sinners were crowded with formal ceremonies'. Among them we get a glimpse of the preparation and dispensing of a hangman's feast, of which no mention is made in the old records. It seems to have been generally permitted to a condemned criminal to spend his last days in feeding himself full. The uses made of this privilege were somewhat varied.

The murderer Gemperlein (1612) would have nothing to do with the wine which was offered to him, but demanded warm herb-beer. In addition the widow of his victim sent him to the prison oranges and gingerbread, ' as a sign that she had forgiven him from the depths of her heart ' (H.). But side by side with moderation and unworldliness, we have many instances of gluttony and wine-bibbing. Thus, according to Magister Hagendorn, Sebastian Gessner (not Gestern, as Master Franz writes) of Giech in the diocese of Bamberg, ' called otherwise in general the Badwastrel ' (H.), thief and house-breaker, ' a fine tall fellow, a soaker and glutton ', who was hanged on 23 July, 1612, ' thought more of the food for his belly than his soul. He is said to have eaten enormously, devouring in one hour a large loaf, and in addition two smaller ones, besides other food '. ' This Sebastian Gessner ', says Frommoder in his report, ' ate so much in the Loch that on the gallows he burst asunder in the middle. The upper part remained hanging and

129

9

the lower part fell down ' (1612). When the homicide Leonhard Deuerlein (1616) was carried on his last journey and was given a drink, he took a long pull at the bottle, drew his breath and said laughing : ' Hi Madela, once again '. When he was reproved by Master Lüder for his conduct, and urged to pray, ' he made answer that he would not pray. We ought to pray since we were paid for it, which I (H.) denied '. Up to the end he preferred to romp with the town watch, desired to pass his water at the place of execution and wanted to drink again. This drink lasted so long that at last the executioner struck off his head while the bottle was still at his lips without his being able to say the words : ' Lord into thy hands I commend my spirit '. ' God have mercy on the poor soul, and pardon those who tempted him to further drinking. . . .' (H.).

After the clerics had done their work, apart from their duty to escort the criminal on his last journey to the place of execution, the principal figure in the picture is the hangman, and after him his assistant, the Löwe. Most of the evil-doers had made their acquaintance in the so-called ' chapel ', the torture-chamber of the Loch prison. From the middle of the sixteenth century to beyond the middle of the eighteenth the principal Nuremberg executioners were Master Leonhard Lippart (d. 1578), and his brother-in-law, the well-known Franz Schmidt of Bamberg who followed him. To Schmidt, when he

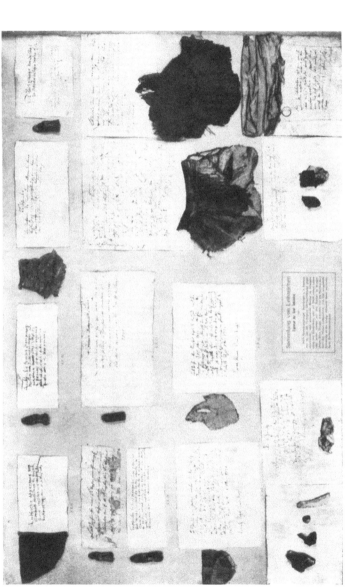

A COLLECTION OF GRUESOME RELICS FROM THE GERMANIC MUSEUM, NUREMBERG

[to face p. 130

gave up his office in 1617, succeeded ' carnifex Bern-hardus Schlegel Amberga oriundus ' (MS. 223, fol. of the Amts-und Standbücher). Then came Valentin Deuster, Mathes Pergner, Johann Conrad Diebler of Amberg, Johann Michael Widemann the elder, Johann Michael Schmid of Windsheim and Johann Michael Wiedemann the younger, who served from 1738 to 1754.

All that is important concerning the position, authority and activities of the executioner and the Löwe (the latter being concerned above all with the unpleasant and superstitious quackeries which I have mentioned) will be found in the writings of Hermann Knapp (see particularly his *Lochgefängnis*, pp. 55ff). It is only possible here to refer to some sidelights of psychological or social interest, and to speak of his relations with the culprits who passed through his hands.

He was announced with the words ' the executioner is at hand ', whereupon he entered and having craved pardon of the condemned persons, he proceeded with the aid of his assistants to bind them. The victims, seized with fear and horror, defiance or penitence, behaved in various ways, as is clear from our sources, as well as from private records. Thanks often to the ministrations of the clerics, some resigned themselves quickly and were self-controlled and penitent in the face of eternity itself, going almost cheerfully to their fate. ' Master Franz, serve me honourably, and I will also behave honourably', so, or in similar words, was the speech to the executioner in the prison or at the place of execution. But at times we are faced with dreadful scenes of despair, with complete collapse or paroxysms of fury, which are in evidence also at times even during the course of the enquiry. Frommoder relates of the highwayman Thomas Ullmann, who was executed with the sword on 14 January 1679 :

'This much be-named Thomas Ullmann, during the course of the honourable enquiry in the presence of a very noble and respected deputy of the council, attacked the executioner in unexpected and sudden manner in the Loch, and beat him cruelly and dreadfully. Without doubt he would have slain him and deprived him of life, had not the gaoler called loudly for help and cried to the guard beneath the Council House, who came quickly and without delay. But this beating cost the said Thomas Ullmann very dear, for he was often brought up and the executioner paid him out in the end '.

Five young men, desperate thieves, had also cause for reflection on 15 December 1615 (compare Meister Franz, p. 78), for some of them when in prison ' had wished Master Franz there so that they might cool their tempers and deal with him in such a manner that he would not speedily forget them. . . .' (H.). The gallows to which, for good or ill, the path was bound finally to lead, were built in 1444, outside the Frauentor, where it remained until the end of Nuremberg's existence as an Imperial city. 'At first composed merely of a rough three-cornered gallows, and a small mound for beheading and breaking with the wheel, it was later transformed into a stately brick erection, in which stood a well-timbered and many-beamed scaffold. By it were poles bearing wheels—a gruesome place. Only the croaking of the ravens broke the silence which was that of a grave-yard '.[1] The main building dates from the year 1578, but in later times there were many alterations and improvements in ' the little church or chapel at St. George's ', as the place of execution was popularly called. The whole carpentering and stone-masons trades had regularly to assist in any work which was necessary, so that none could reproach the others for their share in a shameful and dishonourable task. In what manner the work was accomplished may be gathered from Frommoder's graphic description of the restoration which took place in May 1690 :

'On the third Monday in May (1690) ', he writes, ' the great scaffold or gallows was thrown down by the Löwe, two overseers of the poor and the watchmen, and the following day it was set up again. There marched out with drums and pipes and a few shawms, 168 of the carpenters of the town, among them 16 masters, 10 masters' sons, and 142 apprentices, 109 country masters, 69 stone-masons, and 4 locksmiths' apprentices. When they had marched out they circled the gallows three times, and then commenced to work and build. Six carts or wagons with stone and wood were brought out. On the first cart were 6, on the second, 7 stones ; on the third cart were 5, and on the fourth 4 pieces of timber, and on the two last carts were 24 tree trunks for cross-beams for the scaffold '.

On their last journey to this gallows the poor sinners,

[1] Knapp, *Das Lochfgefängnis*, p. 69.

in the company of the clerics and the upper and lower court officials, came for the first time, often after long weeks and months, into the fresh air and into close touch with their fellow-creatures, for crowds of people assembled in the streets and ways through which the procession passed, and thronged round the Rabenstein to witness the execution. We have already seen how unseemly and turbulent this last journey could be, and how common it was for penitent criminals, who were resigned to their fate and had made their peace with God, to bless the people and beg for forgiveness. It is expressly related of the ' evil thief ' Wolf Bündel (1554), that he blessed also the ' common women ' assembled on the walls of the bastion (M.). We have seen also how the criminals were urged to pray and to turn their minds from earthly things, and how they made short speeches to the people who retaliated with remarks of all kinds. The crowd took sides at times for or against the criminal, but only on rare occasions was any attempt made to interfere with the course of justice. For the most part, cruel as the methods were, we see signs of a healthy popular appreciation of what was fitting. The public knew quite well when to condemn a sordid crime, and when to show pity for the sinner.

We have already heard of Elizabeth, the daughter of one, Schellenclaus who was buried alive, and whose dreadful fate ' so moved the people ' that from that time (1497) this awful punishment was no more inflicted on women. As against this, however, we have an example, in the case of this gold-spinster Schwenderwina, of independent folk-justice, and a few further examples of this nature are given by Knapp in his *Lochgefängnis* (p. 78, but the year date should be 1636, not 1536). I will illustrate one such example a little more fully from Frommoder's report, which may be compared, so far as the offences are concerned (lewdness, procuration, and treason), with Master Franz's account (p. 115), and the version in Siebenkee's Materialien I, 373 (see above). The criminals were married people, Simon and Juliane Schilling (not Schiller).

'On Sunday, the 17 June (1612)', writes Frommoder, 'Simon Schilling, called otherwise generally Boten-Simon, a burgher of this town, and learned in the laws, together with his wife, was beaten out of the town and banished thereafter from the town and district for ever. When they both reached the Frauentor, the woman escaped among the crowd, but him the people stoned as far as the Glockenhof, where he fell down and died. Later the watchmen carried him to St. Peters and buried him.

On 20 June a peasant of Steinbühl, called Hans Körlein, who had stoned the man very grievously with stones, was banished for ever from the jurisdiction of Nuremberg.'

The fury of the populace was always aroused against the executioner and his assistants if, as happened fairly frequently, the execution was unskilfully performed, and the unhappy victim was mishandled, or, as the expression runs, the execution was bungled. We have, for instance, an entry for the year 1506.

'Item, on the eve of St. Martin (10 November), Ulrich Steinmässel was executed for his crimes with the sword.

The executioner, however, did his business so badly that there was an uproar amongst the common people against the executioner, and but for the presence of the town-magistrate, who admonished the people, he would have been stoned to death. Therefore, your honourable council caused it to be announced from the Rathaus on the following Sunday, that, in the future, should the Master chance to be unsuccessful, and execute his victims clumsily, no one under pain of limb, honour, and goods, should raise a hand against him ; which injunction from that time forward was ordered to be publicly proclaimed from the Rabenstein by a town official before each execution, and this was continued until this present time ' (M.).

As early as 1509 when ' the executioner was unskilful there would have been a riot among the common people if it had not been prevented in time '. But in 1540 the failure on the part of the executioner was attributed to the ' inhuman curses ' of the delinquent, and there was therefore no uproar (M.).

If it is desired to obtain a clear impression of the dreadful happenings which occurred at times on the scaffold, it is only necessary to read the description by Frommoder of the execution of the beautiful Margaretha Vöglin, a child-murderer, who was beheaded on 16 March 1641, but sensitive readers would be well advised to skip it. [The description can be read at p. 79 of the German original. It is too dreadful for translation. The executioner was almost stoned to death.] On the following day he [the executioner] was placed in the Loch and relieved of his duties. He was succeeded by Matthes Pergner.

The unsuccessful executions would make a fairly

long list, and to them could be added other examples of lynch-justice, but since these descriptions contain little that is new, I will allow the examples already given to suffice, and add only an account of the final scene which ended all these tragedies.

' The executed criminals, says Knapp (*Lochgefängnis*, p. 77), were either ignominiously buried, or abandoned to the birds of prey on the spot where they paid the penalty for their crimes.' Frequently, however, by permission of the council, they were buried in the unconsecrated portion of St. Peter's cemetery. We hear also at times, after the middle of the sixteenth century, of bodies being appropriated for anatomical purposes. Knapp mentions, as early as 1548, that Magister Heypeln was permitted ' to cut up one of the poor executed victims in St. Peter's church, so long as only a few persons were present '. About the same time, an eye-doctor received a head for purposes of study ' in order that he might the better learn the science ' (Knapp *loc. cit.*).

It appears also, under date 22 February 1571, that on this day ' Erasmus Kühn, brazier and burgher's son of this town, about 20 years old, was executed by favour with the sword on account of his many thefts. The Master did his work unskilfully ; afterwards his body was anatomized '.

Later, it was the custom for the university of Altdorf to ask for individual corpses. Indeed, in time the university seems to have obtained a kind of prescriptive right to them. I give a few examples from the seventeenth and eighteenth centuries.

To his report of the judgment executed upon the assassin Georg Graff (d. 5 November 1672), Frommoder once again adds a ' Nota '. ' This same Georg Graff, upon the repeated request and representations of the students at Altdorf, was placed on a cart at night, carried to Altdorf beforementioned, and there anatomized and dissected.' In the same way, in the case of the ' noxious highwayman ' Hans Wolf (d. 7 April 1685) Frommoder writes, ' Nota : This Hans Wolf was taken down from the gallows at night, placed on a cart, taken to Altdorf and there anatomized and dissected '.

Again we read of the ' determined highwayman ' Hans Eckhard of Leipoldstein (d. 14 December 1717), that ' his body was removed from the gallows at night, and early in the morning it was taken to the Carthusian monastery or Wepsennest, where Dr. Wiedmann anatomized it and made a demonstration to the barber-surgeon apprentices ' (M.). This anatomical demonstration by Dr. Wiedmann is referred to elsewhere in the records.

And just as the clerics concluded their reports with the wish, or the confident hope, that the poor sinner might die like a Christian, so the clerk to the council adds at times a pious text or a little prayer to his entries : ' Requiescant in pace animae '. ' Cuius in domino anima quiescat ', or, in the case of two serious criminals, man and wife (1618), ' Ille vero lachrymans emisit spiritum ; God be gracious and merciful to them both, Amen ' (U.).

But we find nothing of this kind with Master Franz. He closes each year, for the most part, as follows : ' Summa 7 persons ', ' Summa 20 persons ', ' Summa 11 persons ', and finally ' Summa Summarum, all those thus '—in 44 years—' who were executed and brought from life to death, 361 persons : Further those punished in the body and beaten with rods, ears cut off and fingers struck off : 345 persons '.

Chapter IX

ESCAPES

AFTER the horrors which have been paraded before the reader the word ' mercy ' shines out like a mountain peak. There is no word more solemn, more profound, or more divine. But it must be admitted that in the criminal records of past times the quality of mercy did not play a very important part. Too much attention was paid to the letter of the law, which was often extremely harsh in its application, and any departure from the rigorous punishment prescribed was regarded as defeating the ends of justice. The custom which admitted the possibility of intercession did something to alleviate the severities, but we can well imagine what a free pardon must have meant to the tortured victims.

We have seen in many instances what feelings of gratitude were aroused by the mere favour of the sword in place of the rope. Thus Magister Hagendorn reports of ' Hans Dietz of Frankfurt, otherwise the Frankfurt Hänslein, a man of some 24 years, an abandoned thief whose activities were widespread ' (1614), that when ' in response to his supplications and prayers, and in view of his sufferings under torture ', he was granted the favour of the sword, and Magister Hagendorn brought him ' the joyful news that a favourable sentence had been pronounced ', this same Hans Dietz was much restored and comforted, and kissed the hands not only of the clerics, but also of the gaoler, and was ' diligent in his thanks '. As a general rule urgent and weighty petitions were necessary in order to obtain this favour. In the case of the twenty year old thief, who bore the nickname Hahnenmann (1610) not only his family but also his master and the whole of the compass-makers trade, had to use their influence to this end.

As an instance of intercession we may quote the case in 1553 of ' Hans Schwetzer, called otherwise the Ochsenfelder, a watchman on the Inner Laufer Gate, who administered poison to his fellow watchmen ', and was sentenced to death. It was to his good fortune that the old executioner had been sent on leave, and his substitute had not yet arrived, so that the execution had for the moment to be delayed. In the meantime Philip Melanchthon, the honoured founder of the Nuremberg Gymasium, arrived in the town, and as a result of his intercession the criminal was released.

In the same manner, in 1574, the inestuous Michael Steinhauser, was pardoned on the intercession of the Duke of Bavaria, the Palsgrave, and other great lords, who had been set in motion by the criminal's friends. In 1576 the child-murderess Margartha Schüblin was petitioned for by two Polish noblemen and in

1586 two persons guilty of homicide were released by the Archduke Maximilian, who chanced to be present in Nuremberg.

In 1583 Hasdrubal Rosenthaler, a member of a respected family, who had been condemned to death by the sword for serious embezzlements and frauds against his employers, the firm of Fürleger, was respited ' on the weighty petition of the members of the council, and the most eminent among the patriciate ', and was sentenced to life-long imprisonment in the Tower, the cost of which was to be paid by his relatives. ' He remained for more than twenty years a prisoner in the Fröschturm,' says a contemporary chronicler (MS. 18025, fo. in the Library of the Germanic Museum, fo. 98b), 'now, however, 1614, he lives in the Diellinghof (the present Ägidienplatz) in his father's house. He trades and has a wife and child, but may not go out of doors except to church.'

Among the soldiers who in May and June 1553 (that is during the third Margraves' war) were sentenced in the Neuer Bau (the present Maximilians-platz), was one who was guilty of bigamy, and had therefore forfeited his life. ' But since ', so we are told, ' his first wife, and 16 other women besides ', interceded for him, he was reprieved and only beaten out of the town with rods.

In 1606 Hans Scherm, a brazier's son and master-gunner, ' called generally the Duke or the Dutenmaul ', who had been sentenced to death by the sword

for serious silver-thefts, was reprieved on the intercession of a nobleman who lodged in the Bitterholz
(later the Bayerischer Hof on the Karlsbrücke) and
needed a master-gunner. But he soon left the master
to whom he owed his life, and 'is said to have been
executed at Augsburg for theft' (M.).

But at times the council was not in earnest in the
matter of the death-penalty. They relied on the threat
of capital punishment to act as an incentive to the
criminal to repent in terror and fear of death. Feigned
sentences of this kind are met with chiefly in the case
of youthful and childish offenders, as, for instance in
1575, in the case of five young thieves from seven to
eleven years of age, referred to by Knapp (*Das
Lochgefängnis*, p. 75). Their master and companion
was an older thief named Hans Päck, who was hanged
before their eyes, and after they had stood in the
pillory and had been whipped, they were actually
beneath the gallows on the ladder 'and in the very
extremity of terror' (Knapp) before they were reprieved
and banished.

The clerk (MS. 222 fo. Amts-und Standbücher,
Nuremberg State Archives, fo. 61) writes of them :

> 'And although the five little rascals were very cheeky in
> prison, stating even in the pillory that if they had cards they
> would play to see which of them should be strung up first,
> yet when they were carried out they cried bitterly and turned
> round frequently to look at their companions and brothers.
> The one, however, was duly executed. God have mercy on
> his soul.'

In the next year we seem to have a glimpse of a similar proceeding, if we can trust the unofficial report in Murr's manuscript (Pt. II, pp. 20f). On Friday, 3 August, 1576, eight boys, ' evil young rascals who had stolen and cut people's purses ' were before the court.   But as they were ' too young to be hanged ', they were bound together with iron bands, chains, and bells, and forced for a time to sweep the town pavements.   And finally we must mention the fifteen-year-old thief called Hänslein Hoffmann, who (1607) had been several times punished with fear of death and then released.   ' We then ', writes Magister Hagendorn, ' by command of the authorities greatly sharpened the law, since we knew that the proceeding was only a show so that he might be frightened out of such like crimes, but we were forbidden by the authorities to disclose the matter, lest it might appear that we were joking and making child's-play, and that the thing was a sham   .   .   .'

To these official respites and reprieves belong also escapes by force, attempts at flight, breach of prison, and suicide.

In considering this subject, if I desired to preserve a chronological sequence, I could begin early enough with a more or less legendary history of the well-known robber-knight Ekkelein, called commonly Eppelein von Gailinger[1], who lived at the close of the fourteenth

[1] [Ekkelein was sentenced to death, but as a last favour was allowed to embrace his favourite horse. He then sprang into the saddle and leapt over the castle wall into the moat. The hoof marks of the horse are still shown.]

century. But I must confine myself to a few examples which reflect the social conditions of the times.

During Lent of the year 1505, according to the Malefactors' Books (M., part II, pp. 13ff), a needle-maker, one N. Engel, was placed in the pillory for offences which are not specified, the sentence being that his eyes were to be thrust out. 'Then the executioner began to play the fool with him, but he called silently upon St. James, to whom he had already vowed a pilgrimage, and leaping off the pillory, he jumped down and mixed with the people in St. Sebald's churchyard. Then he ran down the long stone steps and through the Schuftergass to the Augustines in their monastery (where he was entitled to sanctuary), and thus he saved his eyes.'

The story of the versatile and expert Hans Reintein is also dramatically related. I reproduce it as follows :

'In the year 1578, on 20 June, at night, Hans Reinla, of Kirchensittenbach, who was by trade a bricklayer, stone-mason, whitewasher and half a carpenter (how this combination was possible is not clear) lying in Nuremberg, in prison for theft, broke out of the Loch in wonderful and cunning manner through a passage, and escaped. He was to be judged on the following Saturday, that is on the morrow of that same day, at a sitting of the council, and condemned to death. It happened in this manner. As is customary, a watchman had been ordered to look after the thief, but he was an old man, called Hans Kob, who had previously been an usher, and he was to watch and take charge of him. When this good old man, on the Friday night, had to watch for an hour he had already had a drink. The thief observed this, and the good old man became somewhat sleepy and his light

145

was extinguished. Possibly the thief had put it out himself. Then the old man tried to ignite it again, but the thief said he might leave it alone, there was no need to light it, since he had better rest and sleep a while, and he (the thief) would do likewise until morning broke. . . . The good old man trusted his words and slept away in the dark. When the thief saw that the old man was asleep he made himself ready, took the light which had been extinguished, and went out of the prison and locked the door, so that the old man was locked in. When the thief was outside he kindled his light from another prisoner's light. Now there was a passage in the Loch which had been made several years ago. It goes under the earth through the Rathaus, and thence under St. Sebald's churchyard, then under the old Milkmarket (to-day Albrecht Dürer-Platz) to the Tiergartner Gate. In it lay the pipes leading to the Rathaus spring. This passage, which the thief helped to make himself, had a hole and an iron door, which always stood open because the season was hot and close, and otherwise it was very stuffy in the Loch. The gaoler had opened it so that the air from the Loch could escape. When the thief saw that this passage was open, and realized his opportunity, since he had helped to make it himself, he went into it and looked about to see if there was anything he could take with him. Now there was an iron lever which was lying inside, and this he took, and with it he broke down first an iron door which he carried along with him. When he thought that he was beneath St. Sebald's churchyard, between the clergy house and St. Moritz's chapel, he made a platform in the passage with the door so that he could reach the roof of the passage with his lever, and began to work at it above his head, hammering and picking until he had made a hole. Then he removed some bricks, so that they fell down into the passage, and made a hole through the roof to the street, big enough for him to crawl out through, and thus he escaped somewhere between the 2nd and 1st hour before dawn, for the watchman who calls the hours passed that way at the 3rd hour before dawn, and at that time no hole was to be seen.

Now the old man, the watchman, when he awaked and

saw that his prisoner had escaped, became very alarmed. Also he was locked in the prison and could not get out, but he made such a to-do that the gaoler's people got up. Then the matter was disclosed to the gaoler, and he informed your honourable council. When the council was aware of what had occurred they allowed the old man, with not a little displeasure, to retain his post as watchman, until the truth had been ascertained, and it was seen whether the old man had assisted the prisoner. But this did not appear, and he accordingly escaped without any penalty. It was supposed that this thief knew how to eat something more than bread, for all the other prisoners declared that never since they had been in the Loch had they slept so softly and soundly as on that night when he broke out. He is said to have escaped from prison in another place, and to have stolen and got away. In summa : he was a cunning and·artful thief.'

Another crafty rogue was Hans Ramsberger, a wire-drawer and spy of the Margrave who was obviously never at a loss, or, as our chronicler puts it, he could eat something more than bread. ' Since he was the Margrave's intelligence-agent' so we learn from the same Manuscript (M.), ' and had betrayed poachers and others' acting thus as informer to the council, ' he was removed on 22 April 1583 from the Loch in Nurenberg, and confined in the Water Tower, for he had taken money from the Margrave, and had been captured in Nuremberg. After he had been in the tower for a while, your honourable council required that certain master wire-drawers should find him work, whereby he might earn something and help to pay·a part of his debts.' Then, to cut the matter short, out of the wire provided by the master tradesmen, and with the aid of his tools, he constructed a ladder which is described in detail by our chronicler ('it had 23 rungs, and each rung was made of nine-fold wire worked into the wood in a most marvellous fashion'), and with this he escaped from the tower. 'But it so happened that in a few weeks be was again captured by the Nuremberg watch, and taken first to the Loch and afterwards again to the tower. Here again he was given work to do, but he would not employ himself, preferring rather to die of hunger. Finally, he was pardoned by your honourable council and set at liberty. But he had to swear that he would not leave the town but remain in it and labour diligently. He did not keep his oath, however, but betook himself again to the Margrave, where he was once more employed as a spy.'

Five years later fate overtook 'this outcast, and thrice-perjured burgher' after he had been guilty of many traitorous acts against his birthplace. He was taken close to Eltersdorf, and beheaded on 28 May 1588. 'The body was quartered, each quarter was hung at a corner of the gallows and the head was stuck on a pole.' A pen drawing, possibly from the hand of the well-known writing master Paulus Frank, in the Official Halsgericht and Urgichtbuch (MS. 223 fo. of the Amts-und Standbücher, fo. 28a) reproduces the scene.

As this criminal, after his second capture and consequent closer confinement, in refusing work and sustenance, seems for a time to have considered the possibility of suicide, so many other victims have sought death at their own hands rather than face the rope, the sword, or the wheel. We hear of one delinquent who, during torture, sought to blow himself out to the last

possible limit in the hope of breaking a blood-vessel in the body or head. But we have few records of actual and successful suicides, although, from the cases cited in this chapter, it is evident that the supervision of the prisoners must have been quite inadequate. Un-doubtedly the majority were gravely concerned for their souls, and were deterred by the thought that any interference with the ways of providence and the course of justice would consign them to everlasting perdition. Such a deed of desperation is quoted as an example by Magister Hagendorn in the case of the suicide of the goat-thief, Hans Beer of Gersdorf, near Bayreuth, who with his associate Michael König (compare Meister Franz, p. 78), was to be executed on 14 December 1615. Three days previously he hanged himself in the night in the Loch ' with a garter which was like a cradle-band '. ' His body was dragged out and thrown to the gallows, where it belonged.'

Chapter X

GALLOWS' HUMOUR

In all the foregoing chapters, as well as in the quotations from the official and private records, in spite of the horrors presented, we are conscious at times of a faint but insistent suggestion of irony, if not of humour. A careless or indifferent attitude on the part of those concerned, like the aversion from suicide, may well have been bound up with the religious belief that the earthly pilgrimage was nothing but a short period of trial, an approach, as it were, to eternal life.

This attitude was strengthened by the harshness of the times, by the continual feuds and warfare, the insecurity of roads and highways, the robberies, attacks, and plunderings, and by the appalling punishments with which the law sought to safeguard society from within and without. With torture and executions as daily occurrences, the sense of horror must have become deadened, and criminals, judges and the public at large saw no cause to restrain their humour or raillery whenever an odd or comic situation arose, which indeed happened not infrequently.

As far as we are concerned to-day, the blunt and picturesque language in which the happenings are related often serves to veil the horrors, but we must remember that it was just this rough and ready mode of expression which at times set fire to the smouldering ashes of discontent.

Thus for instance in 1577 Fritz Kreuzer of Ühlfeld in the Aisch district, a man of thirty-one years, had a difference with ' Mosche, a jew of Fürth ', but he could get no satisfaction from the local bailiff, whereupon he transferred his grievance to an official of Brandenburg-Anspach.   This official threatened, if he did not leave him in peace ' to put him somewhere where the gnats could not get away with him '.   This was sufficient to raise a feud between the man and the communities of Fürth, Dachsbach, Ühlfeld, Holfeld, Tennenlohe and so on, and finally, after sending ' threatening challenges and levying contributions under threats of pillage ', Kreuzer was executed with the sword at Nuremberg on 23 January 1578. ' He remained an unrepentent ne'er-do-well up to the end. Notwithstanding repeated admonitions he would forgive no one ; he would not partake of the holy communion ; he declined to pray on the way out, but cried out continually against injustice, and hoped that the hail would rain down destruction ' (M.).

The incendiary and thief Utz Schöner of Eschenbach (1595) threatened his neighbours that if they did not find 50 or 60 gulden, ' he would throw down another pack of cards at their doors ', by which, says the clerk to the council in his official register, ' he clearly showed his disposition to what was evil '. In a case of attempted poisoning and unchastity (1604) the husband

ILLUSTRATION OF PROVERB
"HE MAKES MUSIC IN THE PILLORY"

Pieter Brueghel, Kaiser-Friedrich Museum, Berlin

[to face p. 152

whom the adulterous couple attempted to remove, says among other things that once at Gostenhof his wife made gruel for him, after partaking of which ' he spewed like a dog '—' to write it decently ', adds the clerk, and Frommoder, full of bitter irony, writes after describing the execution of the blasphemer Hans Hees on 16 October 1660 : ' Nota : This 16 October is said to have been the 22nd birthday of this sinner. He celebrated it very merrily '.

Comic situations were not infrequent and were appreciated by the reporters. The humour is perhaps less apparent to us when we read in the case of the murderess ' Margaretha, the wife of Hans Pecken, carpenter ' (compare Meister Franz, p. 10 for the year 1580), that she attracted her victim, Christina Zahlmeisterin, to her with the promise to comb the lice from her hair. ' Whereupon ', says the woman in her statement, ' she loused her, but matters turned out badly, for anger does much, and she, the speaker, was there four times a week to get her money. . . .'

We have already heard something in Chapter I of the two thieves Hans Ulrich of Heroldsberg and Benedikt Felbinger, and their unrestrained joy and gratitude at being granted the favour of the sword (1614). This joy and confidence remained with Felbinger to the end, and in this mood he set out on his journey to the execution place. As they passed the church of St. Clara, he called out to his companion ' " Hensla, give me a kiss. I will give you one back ", but Hensla remained silent and would not ' (H.).

There is a humorous touch which cannot be restrained, even in the face of tragedy, in the description of three thieves after a murder in the Tetzel chapel in the Church of St. Ägidien (compare above, p. 127), for the youngest murderer did not want to mount the scaffold first, explaining that he would like to see how the thing was done : 'item, the seniors should have precedence', and so on (H.). Another specimen of gallows' humour is reported in the description of the last journey of the two brothers Jakob and Hans Hetzer, tinkers of Fürth, and church thieves (1571), 'two hard heads', who behaved impudently and with great abandon, Hans being 'a lewd fellow', and impudent enough to give vent to an overloud huzza.

To this type of wild humour belongs also the story (1557) of the 'comely young trooper, Claus Meth of Lüneburg', who had been a prisoner of war in Italy, and returning to Nuremberg, had stabbed a companion, also a trooper, during a quarrel in the inn called the Blue Bottle. He was sentenced to death with the sword and was quite willing to die, remarking only, 'Now I have got myself out of Italy, and am once again well suited'.

I have dealt with these half-comic or tragi-comic scenes and happenings in my essay : " Die Nürnberger Malifizbücher als volkskundliche Quelle " [The Nuremberg Malefactors' Books as folklore Sources], see above, p. 21, and I must content myself with one further example, although of course many others could be given.

This is the non plus ultra of wild, arrogant and unrestrained buffonery, presented by the case of the thief Georg Merz of Gibitzenhof, as reported by Magister Hagendorn. I have referred to the affair in Chapter I, and now add in conclusion the description by the notary Georg Frommoder, so that the two accounts may be compared.

'Nota : This Georg Merz, when he left the Rathaus, would not stir a step of the way, but the gaolers were obliged to bring a chair and carry him in it to the place of execution. On the way he kicked the gaolers so cruelly with his feet that they cried out, and frequently let him fall. At the same time he pulled silly faces, bared his teeth to the people, and thrust his tongue far out of his mouth, and played so many foolish tricks that the same can hardly have been heard or seen in the case of any poor sinner before or after. When he reached the accustomed execution place, and the executioner or hangman told him to climb the ladder, he replied : " Why are you in such a hurry with me ? All times are good for hanging, morning, or afternoon, late or early. It helps to pass a dull hour ". And when he was on the ladder and Magister Hagendorn spoke to him, asking him to whom he was going to commend his poor soul, he gave a mighty leap and bursting into laughter, he cried out aloud : " Parson, what is all this talk ? To whom else than to my pot companions, the rope and the chains ? " And when both priests went on to speak comforting words, and called to him to exhort him with their answers, he cried out to them : " I should like to work my jaws much more, but I cannot do so. You can see that I have swallowed a lot of hemp and am like to be suffocated with it, so that I cannot go on talking ". Finally he died stubbornly and in all his weighty sins.'

And so this Satyr's drama can be ended.

CONCLUSION

NOTWITHSTANDING the various aspects and motley colours of the events which have been related, varying from sombre tragedy to wild hilarity, the effect produced by this study of the old Nuremberg criminal classes and their judges is still one of considerable unity, and the reader who has followed us this far is not to be blamed if he finds the material a little monotonous.

But it was not my intention to write a historical romance, and no reader can be expected to devour this book at a sitting; hence the division into ten fairly complete sections. My aim has been to codify the more important aspects of social history as presented in the Nuremberg Malefactors' Books, but so similar are the records at times that they might appear to concern themselves with the fate of one single human being. This defect must be attributed largely to the uniformity, and above all to the inflexibility of the popular conceptions of justice. That ideas in general were bound up not with earthly, but with eternal interests, is clear from the instances we have given. Errors, sins and crimes had to be expiated by the severest and most pitiless punishments. In this the judges, the officials, the criminals, and the great and apparently homogeneous mass of the people were on the whole agreed. Their attitude was almost that of the savage tribe in Central Africa, among whom the punishment decreed for open and acknowledged offences was regarded as the legal privilege of the wrongdoer, which served to cleanse him from his sins.

This sense of righteousness, which survived all the horrors, prejudices and superstitions of the old criminal jurisprudence, influenced, as it was, at times by political considerations, is apparent in the famous reply of the council of the Imperial city to a prince who, in 1452, protested against what seemed to him to be a too rigorous persecution of freebooters, highwaymen and such-like individuals. ' We are not slow when we get to grips with such folk and are able to catch them. If we find them guilty we punish them according to their deserts. If they are innocent we set them free under an oath of peace. It were dearer to us that ten guilty persons should escape than that an innocent person should be put to death.' (Knapp, *Das Lochgefängnis*, p. 29.)

It is due to this earnest and concientious conception of the state's duty and the requirements of justice that we have scarcely a trace of a judicial murder during the time of Nuremberg's existence as an Imperial city. At the worst the case which has been frequently studied of the two half-mad thieves and child-murderers, Maria Eleonora Schönin and Anna Dorothea Härlin (1716), might be so considered, for they retracted their confessions on the scaffold, but were nevertheless promptly executed by order of the town magistrate who had been summoned to the spot.

No less important were the active efforts of the officiating clergy charged with the care of the criminals. They strove by every means to move them to penitence and sorrow, and to some extent to a complete resignation and acceptance of the sentence passed upon them, a state of mind which implies a certain stoutness of heart and mental vigour. A good deal might be said, whether good or bad, concerning the administration of criminal justice in the past—one has only to think of the hosts of abnormal and mentally afflicted criminals, to whom no consideration whatever was shown. But observations, deductions, and practical applications of this kind must be left for future investigation.

CRIMES AND PUNISHMENT OF BARBARA SCHLÜMPFIN

(From the Memorial of M. Joh. Hagendorn)
(p. 250 of Murr's Manuscript)

THE 14 October (1620), Saturday, Barbara Schlümpfin, widow of the honoured and respected burgher and tradesman of this town, Hans Schlümpf of St. Gall, was condemned for her excessive lewdness, adultery, and incest committed during many years with various persons of low and high degree, particularly with a strange trooper now here in the garrison, Heinrich Reinicken of Bremen, to whom she wickedly prostituted her daughter, Sabina Schlümpfin, as appears hereafter from the copy of the judgment which was pronounced.

When I was requested to go down to visit her after Vespers, the council having risen at the service bell, and both prison magistrates, namely Master Ulrich Grundherr, who was thereto specially deputed and ordered by one of the honourable councillors, and Master Hans Friedrich Löffelholz, with the town magistrate, having immediately after the rising of the council descended into the Loch, I commenced her conversion *a lege*, or according to the Ten Commandments, and admonished her as she well deserved, especially from the 18th and 20th chapter of Leviticus, and Deuteronomy 27, opening her eyes to her sins and misdeeds, and reading these words to her from the beautifully illustrated Bible which she had with her in prison :

'And the man that committeth adultery with another man's wife, the adulterer and the adulteress shall surely be put to death. If a man take a wife and her mother it is wickedness and they shall be burnt with fire, both he and they ', etc.

Then I said, ' Hear what you have deserved with your sins if the letter of the law were to be visited upon you, namely fire. And this judgment is not laid down by man, but by God the Lord, himself. I hope, however ', I continued, ' that a gracious judgment may be pronounced.'

With these and similar texts and examples from the New Testament I so softened her heart that she began to weep bitterly, and this continued during the whole period of my first visit.

After I had performed my duty and departed from her I was summoned by the gaoler to attend the prison magistrate and the town magistrate, who were still sitting together at their repast, to make my report as to how the poor sinner had behaved, and whether she was willing to die. This I did and related briefly to their worships what had happened during the past hour between her and me, and at the same time partook of a good drink, in which Master Lüder also joined me.

In the same way, as at the first meeting, I was able to inspire her with fear, sorrow, and sadness, so on the next day I comforted her mightily with the Evangelists, explaining and supporting her with the nine articles of the Christian faith as need arose. When (p. 251) I came to the explanation of the article concerning the burial of our Lord Christ I introduced a digression which the gaoler had suggested to me, and asked if she

had considered whether after her death she wished to be
taken to St. Peter's to be buried, as was usual with the
bodies of people of that kind, or St. John's, where she
had her own grave, and I related to her what had
happened in the case of Dr. Gülcher, and what was
done with him. I explained also that it would be
necessary for her to petition the authorities humbly
in writing. Whereupon she replied that she would
consider the matter.

The day following she caused Master Löscher of the
chancery, who was charged by the authorities with her
matter, to be sent for. To him she disclosed her last
will and what she wished to be done and arranged after
her death. He set down her wishes in his tablets, and
later wrote out the document, and laid it before your
honourable council, with whose approval and consent
her testament was later completed and sealed by
Doctor Herdesiano and Master Gugel, the senior clerks
of the treasury. She then communicated with her
father-confessor, Master Lüder, and arranged for
him to have six gold pennies, but me she excluded
because I did not soften the law, but told her that
according to Holy Writ she had, by her heavy sins,
merited death by fire, which thing I regarded as of
small account, for it was her, not her goods, that I
strove for.

In the afternoon, when I went down to her, I found
her at her repast and had to sit at the table by her,
but I ate little or nothing, drinking only a small
glass of wine. During this hour there was not
much speech concerning God's word, as the woman
gaoler was present as her guest, and we talked of other
matters.

When I went down to her on the last day, I heard
that Master Lüder was already with her and had had
lengthy speech with her in her cell before she was

161

11

brought to the room where I waited, which thing was not customary. When she came in I commenced to comfort her with the first article of our common Christian faith, which I expounded to her as occasion arose. Then Master Lüder commenced to comfort her with the second article, which lasted so long until Master Bernhard (Bernhard Schlägel, the executioner) arrived to secure her, at which she showed no sign of fear or horror, and suffered herself without resistance to be bound as he wished. She was secured like any other poor sinner, except that instead of rope they used taffeta cords.

When we came to the court and she was sentenced to death she enquired whether she should bless their worships, whereupon I said ' Yes, and express thanks also for your gracious sentence '. But she grew dumb and said no word, and thus we departed with her, leaving their worships unblessed.

She remained quiet on the way out and said little or nothing, but looked down until step by step we reached the execution place. When she disrobed she requested that after her death she should be left in her clothes. She asked also that they would be gentle with her, for the Löwe had hurt her somewhat in stripping off her garment at the neck.

When we ascended with her and she should have begged the spectators for forgiveness, I said the words to her, but could not hear that she repeated them, so softly did she speak in everything she said. Therefore I repeated the Lord's Prayer in a loud voice in her stead. Then I reminded her that she should commend her soul to God, her creator, who had redeemed her through Christ, His beloved son. And while I spoke to her thus and the executioner was disrobing, she looked round and begged him for the love of God to suffer her before her end to speak a word, which was permitted and she rose up from the chair. But when we drew nearer, intent on hearing what she might say, she once again became dumb, as she was before the court, and could speak no word. Then she was once more placed in the chair, but when the executioner was now ready to strike she looked round again, so that he could not complete his stroke, but had to drop his sword behind the back of the chair on which she sat. Finally the Löwe had to hold the head with one hand and the eye-bandage with the other. Then the executioner struck with all his force, but because she drew in her shoulders he struck too high, so that the head remained hanging by the skin, but with another stroke he severed it as she lay on the ground.

Soon after she, or rather her body, when it had bled a little, was taken by the overseers of the poor from the Rabenstein and placed in a wooden coffin overlaid with pitch, on which was placed also the black woollen cloth on which she had been executed. The coffin was then closed and carried to St. Peter's, where it lay for half a day until after the closing of the gates. Then the grave-digger and his assistants returned and carried her thence to St. John's, and laid her in a new grave which had been prepared by the deceased Schlümpf, and which, as she told me, had cost more than 60 florins. But the honourable epitaph placed there was torn down by order of the authorities.

She was in truth a great sinner, and had committed her horrible crimes for twelve whole years. But since she had found grace in time and had done penance, and had (p. 253) heartily deplored and wept over her sins, I hope that God will have pity on her as he did on that other poor sinner, Mary Magdalen, and pardon her her grievous sins, which were washed away by the rosy blood of Christ, and receive her into everlasting joy and splendour. God grant her on the great day of the

Lord a joyful resurrection in the name of Jesus Christ His son.

Now follows a copy of the judgment pronounced.

Whereas your honourable council of this town, by office and authority [have duly examined] Barbara Schlümpfin, who for the following sufficient reasons was first carried to the tower Lugisland, and then to the Loch prison, for that she in many ways, in despite of God's holy word and his holy Sacraments, had during the time of her lawful marriage spent her days in wanton, goodless, and guilty living. Not only had she, during her married life with Daniel Schlümpf and during her widowhood [here follows an account of her adulteries and her lecherous dealings with her daughter], well knowing that she was committing incest against all the laws of God, man, and nature, and in great contempt and scorn of Christian discipline and honour, and above all of God's holy institution of marriage, all which same offences were acknowledged before the holy Imperial judge and two sworn magistrates, by the said Barbara Schlümpfin, with other details and circumstances, she being free, unconstrained and unbound, so that the matters became known and open, whereby she came within the penalties of the prescribed Imperial laws and of the Imperial criminal code, and had forfeited life and limb.

Therefore it was adjudged by my lords and the magistrates sworn to administer the law, that the said Barbara Schlümpfin had well deserved earthly punishment and that, as an example to others that they might the better know how to avoid such culpable offences in the future, therefore the said Barbara Schlümpfin shall be carried to the customary place of execution, there by special grace to be executed with the sword and brought from life to death as an evil-doer. All this according to law.

Frommoder (fo. p. 61) reproduces the words of this judgment and reports the unsuccessful execution in a nota : ' Because this Barbara Schlümpfin, on account of her great fear, terror, and horror, did not hold herself properly she was badly executed by the executioner, Bernhard Schlägel, and her head was sawn and cut off as she lay on the ground '.

EXECUTION AT BRESLAU ON 23RD JANUARY
1654, OF HEINRICH THEIN, WHO HAD
COMMITTED 251 MURDERS

(After Frommoder, fo. 143a)
Anno 1654

MONDAY, 23 January, a dreadful murderer named
Heinrich Thein, who had been a watchman, constable
and bailiff, was executed at Breslau in the following
manner, because he had during his confinement
acknowledged that he had committed 251 cruel murders
apart from the soldiers whom he (presumably in war)
had slain and not spoken of or noticed. First his four
members, that is hands and feet, were pinched, then
he was torn in four places, on chest and arms with
red-hot irons, after which he was dragged to the
gallows on an ox-skin. There he was broken with the
wheel on a platform which had been prepared, and
then quartered, the four quarters being set up on the
highway. This evil-doer was so patient that he did
not once cry out, nor did he do anything or conduct
himself unmannerly. I saw him executed with my
own eyes.

SOME NAMES OF THIEVES AND ROBBERS
FROM THE SECOND HALF OF THE
SIXTEENTH CENTURY

(This is, of course, largely concerned with nicknames)

On 26 November 1555, Hans Hoffmann, a young butcher's son, called der Zwifeltreter was beheaded for rape (M.). In 1578 numbers of thieving bands were dispersed and many of their members were executed. One of the leaders was Heinz Pirger of Heindsdorf, near Wolfsberg, a swine-herd. He said of himself during the enquiry that he was called der lange Stark (the long strong one), and also Hafel-Heinz. At Hersbruck he called himself Heinz Peer, since his godfather, who had been a Landsknecht, was also so called. But after his father he was called Heinz Pirger. . . .' Among his companions were: der Schickende Hermann: Class of Pommelsbrunn: Klein Willibald (Little Willibald) and die Maus (the Mouse); Georglein Falk, called der Pfeiferlein (Little Piper); Schmir Ulein; Schwarz Michel (Black Michel). Of the last we are told: '. . . About half a mile below Pretzfeld Black Michel laid himself down to rest beneath a great tree, called the thieves' tree, where the thieves used to meet . . .'
    In the proceedings against the thief Michel Krauss, called otherwise Schlotterer, a peasant, who was hanged

on 26 July 1578 at Hersbruck, the following names of 'infamous highwaymen and wicked scoundrels' appear:

One called der Göcker; Zigeuners Closs (Gipsy Closs); Klein Willibald (Little Willibald, see above); one called der Anferlein; Lienhard of Schwandt; der Sandhas; der Hellgarten; Schicklet Hermann (see above); Stark Heinz (Strong Heinz), Lemlein, also Lemblein (the Little Lamb); Pelzfleck, otherwise Bastlein; Schwarz of Dornitz; Steffan of Ofenhausen; Stumpf Henslein, and his brother Martin; Kuh-Heinz (Cow-Heinz); Bonlein (Koseform of Pankratz) of Schimmerndorf; two young girls, among them the one called Thomas Künlein, and the other Cappel Ännlein (the Christian names are mostly placed second); der Hundsdorfer; one called Lubschneider; Pfeifer Peter (Peter the Piper); Dick Henschlein; Heffner, or Schefer, of Schesslitz; der Pengel, called otherwise Cunz; das Percktmendlein (also Pirckmendlein); Lang Schwab; Gross Frank (Big Frank); Küchenhenslein; Lungslein (also Lüngslein); Lindenmair; one called the Pehaimschen Bauer (the Bohemian peasant).

From the proceedings against the thieves Hans Pankmann of Kunstett and Jorg Rumpf (executed 7 Oct. 1578); Der Spreckelte (also Sprecklet, etc.); Schwarzferberlein; Henslein Wisch (A.).

From the proceedings against the thieves Lienhard Walz, otherwise Lienla of Schwendt (see above), Peter Mulner and Hermann Schrötel (executed 2 August 1580) many of those already named appear with der gatzete Mehchior; Schwarzen Wölfle; Jorg of Gebirg; Schnellgattern; Jorg mit dem bösen Kpof (with the evil head); Pappenhaimer; Schmir Ule (see above); Jorg Pfeufer mit dem lahmen Arm (with the lame arm) (A.).

In the same year 1580 I may mention Saffranmennle (the little saffron man); die Feuerkugel (the fire-ball); Jorg Hist, called otherwise Richtnitter of Sützkirchen (?); Martin Herdegen, Hennen-Martin of Schwarbach; Hans Humbser of Lamprechtshofen, called otherwise Adam (A.).

1581 : der feiste Michel; Pappen Mertl; feist Cunz; Gatzet Lienle; Hensle and Matl, called die Gottlanger; der Hinkende Schuster (the limping shoemaker), called Hans; der Grosskopfet (Big-head); Jorg Stirer, called Knaup and Sailer; der Kittel.

1582 : 'Kadra (probably Katharine, written also Kathra, Cathra) Buckin, called otherwise 'stammering Kadra', whose father was called Hans Teutsch and was born in Vienna', highway-robber and burglar, 'with her company, infamous and bloodstained in the districts of Würzburg and Eichstätt' (executed 20 February 1582). To her band belonged 'the naked one, a pale, washed-out fellow, going about in rags. He wore an old, white, woollen shirt, with an old doublet over it, linen trunk-hose, with linen stockings, and carried an old staff with him; the great Roller, a fat fellow without a beard, with a red face, dressed in white like a miller. He wore an apron, a white hat, and carried a weapon in a sheath'. The other members of this band are similarly described (A.).

1584 : 'Ketterle Schwarzin of Wehrd (Wöhrd, near Nuremberg), a thief and begging whore' (executed 11 Feb. 1584. Compare Meister Franz, p. 14; [English translation, p. 125]). The thieves' company consisted of : Hensle of Geiselwind, called also Klein Dick (Little Dick); Ula or Ule; Klein of Bamberg; Hensle Baldauf, called Siechenhensle; Pulferle; Schwoble; Knappet; Kilian Wurm of Virnsberg, and Hans Klopfer of Reichelsdorf; also the ladies : Steinfelderin; Margarethe; Maria; Spitzkopf; Sebele (A.).

In 1585 there are named : Stumpfle ; Zahnlucket Fritz (? Teethless Fritz) ; Kopp of Alfeld, called otherwise Strohbub (Straw-baby) ; Ule of Bohenstrauss ; Mertl Fridl of Pilsen ; Seufride of Flos (A.).

1588 : der Seusack ; der gelbe Cunz (Yellow Cunz) ; Hirten-Liendl (Shepherd-Liendl) ; der Krank ; der Spracht, and many others.

1594 : der gross Vilsecker (the big Vilsecker) ; der Knödel ; der Bueb (the Boy) of St. Ela (?).

1600 : Georg Mörzelein of Gradenberg, vagabond and thief, called otherwise der Dölp (compare Meister Franz, p. 52). Executed 12 Feb. 1600 (A.).

NUREMBERG INNS, BEER-SHOPS AND TAP-ROOMS

THE Golden Goose, 1557 (M.); The Blue Key, near the White Tower, 1557 (M.); The Blue Bottle, 1557 (M.); The Ox-Meadow (later The Three Kings) in the Neuer Bau (now Maximiliansplatz), 1562 (M.); The Golden Cross on the Upper Füll, 1574 (M.); the host of The Golden Hatchet behind St. Jakob; the Kürschner Inn, 1576, and 1597 (MS. 18025, fo. in the Library, Germanic Museum); the host of the Seven Towers, 1577 (ebenda); The Boot, 1579, where the Landsknechts foregathered (A.); The Oak, 1579 (A.); the host of the Lamb, 1580 (A.); ' Berlehuetter ', 1580 (MS. 18025, fo. see above); Niklas Schätzl, host on the Stone Bridge (now Maxbrücke), at the corner-house called the Millstone, d. 1580 (ebenda); The Red Cock near St. Lorenz, 1582 (ebenda); The Little Gold Post-Horn, 1584 (M); The Five Towers, outside in the Schmiedgasse, 1584 (A.); The White Lion near St. Jakob, 1586 (M.); the host of The Golden Star, 1589 (MS. 18025, fo., see above); 'In the Kappenzipfel near the Red Ox, opposite the Mehlwag', 1589 (ebenda): the hostess of The Golden Crown in the Beckschagergasse, 1590 (ebenda); The Plow, a hostess of The Golden Table, near the Kalkhütten (near St. Ägidien) was beaten with rods in 1595 (ebenda); Ursula Brummin, hostess of The Red Deer, in the

Lorenzer Platz, 1594 (M.) ; The Moor's Head, 1598 (A.) ; The Owl, 1615 (H.) ; the host of The Red Horse, 1617 (A.) ; The Blue Bottle (see above), in the Kohlenmarkt (now Josephsplatz), 1619 (H.) ; the host of The Little Cow beneath the White Tower, 1620 (H.) ; the host of The Moor's Head (see above) at Wöhrd, 1662 (F.) ; the hostess of The Little Cask at Wöhrd, 1662 (F.) ; The Red Horse (see above), 1665 (M.) ; the host of The Golden Bear, 1675 (M.) ; The White Lamb in the Füll, 1679 (M.) ; the tavern of the Grape, here on the Steig, 1692 (M.).

INDEX

INDEX

*For Product Safety Concerns and Information please contact
our EU representative GPSR@taylorandfrancis.com Taylor & Francis
Verlag GmbH, Kaufingerstraße 24, 80331 München, Germany*

T - #0127 - 270225 - C0 - 218/133/12 - PB - 9780815368908 - Gloss Lamination